Published by
ACADEMIC FOUNDATION
in association with

Institute of Public Enterprise

ABOUT THE AUTHORS:

R.K. Mishra, Senior Professor and Dean is the Director of Institute of Public Enterprise (IPE), Hyderabad, is a graduate of International Management Programme, SDA Bocconi, Milan, Italy. He has been a fellow of the British Council and the Commonwealth Secretariat. He has worked on key assignments with Indian government including Ministry of Finance, Ministry of Power, Ministry of Trade and Commerce, Ministry of Heavy Industry and Public Enterprises, and Ministry of Finance (Department of Disinvestment). He has also worked extensively with international organisations including OECD, United Nations University-World Institute for Economic Development Research, International Civil Service Consortium. His current areas of interest include: corporate finance, corporate governance, international management, management controls, management education, infrastructure development, restructuring, economic reforms, social sector management, good governance and economic environment.

Geeta Potaraju is currently working as an Assistant Professor at IPE, Hyderabad. She has a PhD in Management with specialisation on public sector enterprises. She has over 15 years of experience in development consulting. Her areas of interests are: participatory governance, health system strengthening, administrative and institutional reforms. Dr Geeta has been involved in a number of key assignments with DFID, UNDP, World Bank, World Bank Institute, Family Health International, Government of India, and state governments. She is an expert on participatory governance tools like Citizens Charters and Right to Information. She has extensively worked on issues of access to information and has developed training manuals for both the supply side as well as the demand side stakeholders.

Memorandum of Understanding in India

Memorandum of Understanding in India

R.K. MISHRA and GEETA POTARAJU

ACADEMIC FOUNDATION
NEW DELHI

www.academicfoundation.org

First published in 2016
by

ACADEMIC FOUNDATION
4772-73 / 23 Bharat Ram Road, (23 Ansari Road),
Darya Ganj, New Delhi - 110 002 (India).
Phones : 23245001 / 02 / 03 / 04.
Fax : +91-11-23245005.
E-mail : books@academicfoundation.com
www.academicfoundation.com

in association with
Institute of Public Enterprise, Hyderabad.

Disclaimer:
The findings/views/opinions expressed in this book are solely those of the authors and do not necessarily reflect the views of the publisher.

Memorandum of Understanding in India

by R.K. Mishra and Geeta Potaraju

ISBN 9789332703407

Typeset by Italics India, New Delhi.

Printed and bound by The Book Mint, New Delhi.
www.thebookmint.in

CONTENTS

1

Performance Contracting

A Global Perspective

Introduction

In the era of privatisation, the concern for PEs (public enterprises) is right at the top of the policy maker's agenda. This is true particularly for the LDCs (less developed countries) where PEs have spread themselves all over the key sectors of economy. The growth of PEs in these countries is a direct measure of the success or failure of their economies. There is a general belief that PEs have failed to deliver goods, though there is no common view as to why this has happened, although, various alternative measures for the improvement of these enterprises have come up.

Public enterprises have conflicting objectives. Being 'enterprises' they are required to function on commercial lines, making optimal use of the resources—financial physical, material, and human. At the same time, unlike their counterparts in the private sector, being 'public' they have to serve public interest. However private an enterprise may be, it cannot escape its obligations towards the broader public good. Secondly, government as an overall supervisor, can control these enterprises through a number of regulatory measures. This is a specific disadvantage, especially for the developing economies. The government must be conscious of the constraints imposed on PEs. But if the government remains indifferent in this aspect, PEs labour under severe structural handicaps, which endanger not only their performance but also the economy as a whole. This risk is all the greater in economies where the public sector is required to occupy 'commanding heights'.

Concept of Performance Evaluation in Public Enterprises

The year 1967 marks a watershed in the annals of French PEs. This is the year in which the Nora Committee was appointed to inquire into the functioning of PEs and suggest measures for their improvement. The committee submitted its recommendations to the government. The report brought to light the confusion arising out of the excessive control on the PEs by the government. It also brought forth a sense of complacence or apathy, on the part of the different parties involved, towards the efficient functioning of these enterprises. The report called for a classification of government-PE relationship. This report envisaged essentially a two-programme measure (Trivedi, 1968).

i) Increased autonomy to the management of PEs, and
ii) A realistic pricing policy, in order that the units do not have to depend on the government for balancing their accounts.

The programme contract gave a new orientation to the relationship between the state and PEs. It called for a multi-annual programming of the manpower and resources available to the enterprise, following posterior control over *a priori* control. This new orientation brought the PE closer to the management pattern followed in the private firms. Thus, the programme contract came out as an instrument for rationalising the management of PEs.

The programme contract removes PEs from the enclave and returns them to the market economy. It ensures that the management of a PE would be similar to that of a private firm, with the aims of rationality and efficiency. This would mean that the enterprise would know their objectives for the next several years and the financial targets, which it has to reach. This makes long term and medium term planning and programming necessary. Moreover the enterprises should not be burdened by excessive supervision, which would dampen initiative and dilute responsibility. The programme contract serves as a planning tool at two levels (Trivedi, 1968): (i) at the macroeconomic level, it is an additional instrument for national planning, and (ii) at the microeconomic level it constitutes a true business plan.

According to the Nora Report:

> Its purpose is to improve efficiency in the management of the economy by seeking maximum consistency among the plans of individual economic agents. It by no means conflicts with the functioning of the market, rather it improves market action by clarifying it (and thereby permits) retention of context over the objectives of growth (Trivedi, 1968).

As mentioned earlier, the contracts had no standard format. However, a few of them incorporated four essential elements in their contracts, which gave rise to high degree of subjectivity to the contract (Jean-Yvse, 1968):

i) The strategy of PE for a medium term (3 to 5 years), based on the governments macroeconomic perception for the development plan.
ii) Propositions formulated by the enterprises for adopting this strategy to the fundamental goals of the French government's economic policy.
iii) Areas of financial relations with government, especially the financial targets of the enterprise.
iv) The government's obligations to cover the additional costs of non-commercial objectives and relevant procedures for achieving this reciprocal commitment.

The Nora Committee envisaged these measures in the framework of well-defined contracts, which would list out objectives expected to be fulfilled by the PEs as well as the financial assistance to be expected of the government. The contract would also quantify, arising out of its obligations to the public interest and compensate the PE, fully on this count. For the enterprises in the competitive sector, the report envisaged primarily, the establishment of sound management principles in line with their counterparts in the private sector. Thus, were born the first generation of contracts.

Performance Contracting in South Korea

South Korea has a history of embracing capitalist market forces, an industrious labour force and dynamic private entrepreneurs; these are complemented with a government which encourages economic growth through progressive economic policy. And yet surprisingly, the public sector played an important role in the development of a robust Korean industry. The role played by the public sector in Korean economic development was in line with Korean government's commitment to various economic goals, such as export promotion, accelerated development of heavy industry and effective distribution of public utilities (Park, 1968).

The GIEs (government invested enterprises) however, were not successful in achieving the levels of performance that were expected of them. By the late 1970s, the disappointing financial condition of the GIEs and their burden on public resources, dented the reputation of the public sector and became a concern for the Korean public and government. Prior to introduction of the Government Invested Enterprises Management Act in 1984, several factors contributed to the inefficient performance of GIEs in Korea such as (Song, 1988):

i) low rate of return on capital;
ii) increasing number of deficit enterprises; and
iii) excessive government interference in operations of the GIEs.

Extensive government control on enterprises was facilitated through various laws and regulations, such as: Government Invested Enterprise Budget, Accounts Act and Government Invested Enterprise Administration Act. The aforementioned laws were supplemented by special laws, such as, the Government Invested Establishment Act. Government control was leading to inefficiency of Korean PSEs (public sector enterprises); while the importance of government control in the early phases of the enterprises is accepted, such government intervention in the operation of well established enterprises leads to the poor performance of the enterprises. Autonomy is critical in PSEs, because the management must have the confidence to take decisions without fear of intervention by the government officials, which was absent in the Korean PE prior to 1983. Performance of enterprises was also affected by appointments being made on political considerations, instead of managerial professionalism. Multiple principals such as the Line Ministry, Ministry of Finance, Economic Planning Board and Board of Audit, all exercised their respective spheres of influence on the enterprises giving rise to multiple and conflicting objectives. Korean enterprise hence, had to deal with multiple principals and multiple objectives hindering the decision-making of managers, who were unsure as to what the enterprise was expected to do.

Performance Management in Public Sector Enterprises

The PSEs in Korea can be divided into four categories, namely:

i) Government Enterprises.
ii) GIEs.
iii) Subsidiaries companies of GIEs.
iv) Other government backed enterprises.

Korea's significant step for improving performance of PSE came in the form the Government Invested Enterprises Management Act, passed on the 16 December 1984. The legislation had two primary directives, to enhance managerial autonomy, accountability and to exercise effective control. The Act introduced a system of MBO (management by objective); preparation of budgets, for example, was in line with this new system of MBO. The Act also introduced a slew of other changes in policy, such as increasing the autonomy of managers over a range of enterprise operations, like procurements, budgeting and personnel policy. A two-tiered management organisation was introduced, with the board of directors as the decision-making body and enterprise president as the chief executive in charge of implementation. Audits of enterprises from outside were simplified and business supervision by technical ministries was removed. And importantly, an *ex-post* evaluation system with a linked incentive system, was also introduced.

In order for this evaluation system to work and function effectively, several key institutions in the government machinery and in the GIEs had to be fine tuned. The Korean government machinery in place to evaluate enterprise performance is as follows:

- GIE Management Evaluation Council: It is the highest council concerned with the overall management of GIEs. This council formulates general guidelines for preparing the management objectives and budgets of GIEs and evaluates managerial performance of GIEs. The chairperson is the Minister of Economic Planning; the other members are the minister of relevant technical ministries and three temporary commissioners from the private sector.

- Public Enterprise Evaluation Bureau: This bureau functions as the permanent secretariat of the Management Evaluation Council. The director of the bureau is the executive secretary of the council and also the de jure member of the boards of directors of all GIEs.
- GIE Management Evaluation Ad-Hoc Task Force: This task force is given charge of actually carrying out performance evaluation. The members of this task force are experts in their respective fields, such as professors in economics, business administration, experts from research institutes, businessmen and CPAs.
- GIE Special Task Force: The purpose of this task force is to balance the skill, knowledge and expertise between the government and GIE, which is needed for performance evaluation. The task force consists of highly qualified personnel from within the GIEs, so essentially creating a unit within them.
- Sectoral/technical ministries: The interference of the sectoral and technical ministries has been reduced drastically by the Act. The ministries are directed to formulate sectoral policies to be carried out in sync with the national development strategy. The ministries are tasked, therefore, to discuss and reach agreement upon management objectives.

Performance Contract (PC) System (PCS) in Korea

PCS has been implemented in the Korean public sector, since 1984, as a part of the management of SCEs (state-capitalised enterprises). It is a management Performance Evaluation System (PES) (Kwanbo, 2001). In 1999, the law was revised with the objective to increase operational autonomy, accountability and transparency of

SCEs. The measures introduced included abolishing of government appointed board of director and adopting a system of standing and non-standing directors. Recruitment of CEOs of SCEs was changed and recruitment was done by a presidential nomination committee, along with signing of management performance contracts for their jobs. A new management disclosure system was also stipulated under which SOEs were required to reveal management information, such as financial reports and management review over the internet, which was in public interest. Citizen charters were to be introduced by SOEs in order to promote consumer consciousness, regular customer satisfaction surveys were also to be conducted with the same objective. Lastly, several measures to improve efficiency and competitiveness of SOEs were introduced, such as, performance based salaries for senior management, external monitoring of management, knowledge based management systems and EVA (economic value added) system.

Features of the Performance Contracts

i) Increased managerial autonomy over operational aspects such as budgets, procurement and personnel.
ii) Incentivising performance by linking incentives to performance results.
iii) Comprehensive evaluation of performance through selection of specific and multiple objectives.
iv) Implementation of PCs within the organisational arrangements.

Indicators for Performance Evaluation

The PCS system employs two types of indicators for evaluation of performance:

i) Quantitative indicators: These are objective indicators for measuring performance through numerical estimates. Quantitative indicators employ objective-performance, trend analysis, and Beta distribution methods. In the performance over management method, evaluation scores for SOEs range from 0 to 100 points.

ii) Qualitative indicators: Korea utilises a nine-scale grading evaluation method to evaluate the non-quantitative indicators (A+A0, B+B0, C0, D+D0, E+E0). As opposed to quantitative indicators qualitative indicators are evaluated by a sub-group in the ad-hoc task force, by subjective judgement of managerial performance.

An overall performance of the SCE is determined through an aggregate score, which combines both the quantitative and qualitative indicators and multiplies it with their respective weighted values. These evaluations are then required to be submitted to the Ministry

Case Study: South Korea Experience with Performance Evaluation System (PES)

South Korea has a total of 303 institutions which are designated as SOEs under the Act on the Management of Public Institutions (2014.4). The Koreans have experimented and fine tuned their PES over the years and now have a well structured and effective PES for their SOE. The first stage of the broad transition was between the years 1984 and 2003, where the performance, evalution of public corporations was introduced, which included the CEO performance evaluation and innovation evaluation. The second stage of the transition of the performance evaluation system was between 2004 and 2007, when the performance evaluation of quasi-governmental organisations was introduced in addition to evaluation of public organisations, which evaluated the CEO performance, innovation, and auditor's performance. The last stage started from 2008 and continues presently which is the performance evaluation of SOEs system.

The broad monitoring system for SOEs in Korea has two parts. The first part is the performance evaluation system under which the following components of the SOEs are monitored: SOE performance; CEO performance agreement; and evaluation of the senior auditors. The second part of the monitoring of SOEs is the ALIO (All Public Information in One) system, which is a system introduced to increase transparency through an information disclosure system.

The public institutions in Korea are evaluated by the Ministry of Strategy & Finance (MoSF), or the line ministries, depending on the size and profitability of the corporations and organisations. The MoSF evaluates only the bigger public corporation or organisations which have self generating revenue of more than 50 per cent and also qausi-governmental organisations, which have a self generating revenue of less than 50 per cent. With regards to size,the evaluation of the corporations and quasi-governmental organisation is done by the MoSF only in case the total employment is greater than or equal to 50 people. Public institutions (PIs) which are non-classified and have less than 50 employees are evaluated by their respective line ministries. The evaluation of the SOEs is conducted by a Performance Evaluation Unit, which is a temporary team consisting of about 160 experts from varied fields like academics and research analysts, etc. The MoSF also organises an independent team to evaluate the performance. Once the evaluation team evaluates the performance of the PIs the results are finalised by the Committee for Management of PIs. The PIs may also have complaints and policy suggestions which are directed to the Research Centre for State-Owned Entities, which further suggests the system improvements to the MoSF, which go to the committee for management of PIs where they are deliberated and resolutions are passed, and finally the evaluation team approves and finalises the system improvements. The system is based on a balanced evaluation between business administration and core businesses. There are two types of indicators against which performance of the SOEs are evaluated: quantitative and non-quantitative indicators, which are divided on 65 to 35 per cent ratio. For business administration, non-quantitative indicators include strategy planning, financial management, remuneration and welfare benefits, while the quantitative indicators include, business efficiency, government recommending policy. As regards core businesses, the non-quantitative as well as and quantitative indicators include plan activities and performances.

The results of the evaluation are divided into six grades, after they are converted to scores on a 100 scale. The six grades are S (Superior), A, B, C, D, E (inferior). Based on the results of the performance evaluation, the incentive rate is decided. The range of the incentive rate varies from 0 to 250 per cent of the monthly wage, depending upon the grade received in the evaluation. SOE employee's incentives are determined by adding the institutional performance bonus and personal incentives. The Korean system also has a very unique penalty system, where the MoSF, in cases of low rated institutions may recommend the dismissal of CEO.

Presentation made by Mr Wonhee Lee, Director, Research Centre for State Owned Enterprises, Korea Institute of Public Finance (KIPF) at the International Workshop on Performance Evaluation and Management of State Owned Enterprises, January 2015, New Delhi.

of Planning and Budget (MPB), related ministries and the national assembly.

Incentives

The evaluation system is linked to the incentive system (in the form of bonuses). The task force conducts performance evaluation each year and the bonus size varies between 0 per cent and 500 per cent of monthly wages, depending on the evaluation results in the nine categories. The system also incorporates non-pecuniary incentives and sanctions. Awards are handed to the highest scoring enterprises while the enterprises that are performing poorly could face sanctions (e.g., dismissal of top management). Finally, an important part of the entire system, is the wide publicising of the results of the performance evaluation in mass media. Public recognition plays an important role in Korean society and is a powerful motivational tool for performance of top management.

Performance Contracting in Ghana

In Ghana, by the 1980s, the Ghana Cocoa Board along with 16 other enterprises formed the core of PSEs. the Ghana Cocoa Board was a major source of revenue for the state, while the other 16 core PE were in other important sectors such as energy, transportation and communication sectors. However, by the 1970s and early 1980s these core enterprises and their performance started suffering and prompted the public sector reform programme, which was introduced in 1987.

The PCS for PEs was introduced with the start of the PE reform programme in Ghana. The PCS was introduced with the aim of improving the performance of the core SOEs (state owned enterprises). PCs proved to be an important tool for managing interaction between the government and enterprise, while initially it was seen only as temporary and contributing tool for improving performance of the core enterprises. Prior to this period, SOEs governance, both in terms of legal and institutional mechanism, had seen deterioration, coinciding with declining economic development and rising political instability. In 1982, first attempts were made to restore discipline in SOEs governance through the Interim Management Committees

(Public Boards and Corporations) Law. The enactment of the 1982 law meant that the existent SOEs management system through boards of directors was removed, and in its place, Interim Management Committees were put in place. The legislation heralded a period of SOE self management for nearly a decade, in which SOE management was virtually out of the hands of the sector ministries and was in the hands of committees of its own employees. It was in this background that PCs were first signed as, part of the SOE reforms programme in Ghana.

The overall reform programme included tools like PME (planning, monitoring and evaluation) system, which adapts the corporate plan to economic realities, negotiating annual performance objectives and targets; quarterly reporting and annual evaluations. The reforms also included an annual cycle of setting performance objectives between the sectoral ministry and the enterprise; the State Enterprise Commission (SEC) and the Ministry of Finance and Economic Planning also formed party to this annual cycle, thus linking all these stakeholders.

Performance Management in Public Sector

In Ghana, PCS forms part of the PME system. We will take a brief look at the elements of the PME system and its essential features before focusing on PCs. The PME system formed an essential feature of the SOE reform programme, introduced by the government in Ghana in the early 1990s. One of the main functions of the SEC was to manage and implement this system. As mentioned earlier the PME system was introduced as a mainstay to improve the performance of SOEs; the system incorporates three essential elements which are implemented in an annual cycle (Adda, 1994):

i) Updating of corporate plan.
ii) Negotiation of PCs.
iii) Quarterly monitoring and annual evaluation and reporting of performance.

Corporate Plan

The introduction of corporate plans was an important part of the PC system; prior to PCs, corporate plan was not a standard feature in many of the core enterprises. Neither the sectoral ministries nor the enterprise management, had much experience in preparing such corporate plans, and so, external consultants were relied on to prepare the corporate plans. However, using external consultants to prepare corporate plans did not meet with much success, as the sector ministries and the enterprise managers were confused and unable to adapt to these new corporate plans. By the early 1990s, most of the SOE had started preparing their corporate plans without external consultants, but updating corporate plans annually was not common.

Performance Contracts

PCS is a performance enhancing instrument, which is entered into by the SOE management and the sector ministry; the SEC facilitates the negotiating and signing of the performance contracts.

In 1991, the contracts had a standardised format that contained elements such as:

i) Objectives.
ii) Performance indicators to be monitored and annual targets to be achieved during the contract period.
iii) Mutual undertakings of government and enterprise.
iv) Critical arrangements made in setting targets and reporting requirements.

PCs set targets and objectives, which are mutually agreed upon by the enterprise managers and the concerned ministries. Specific indicators are used to measure the performance of the SOEs against the objectives and targets in the PCs. In Ghana these targets are set under four main themes, such as (Simpson, 2013):

i) Financial/economic.
ii) Efficiency/productivity.
iii) Dynamic effects.
iv) Management improvements/projects.

However, at the time of evaluation of performance, the targets are categorised again, into three themes: (i) financial/economic; (ii) dynamic effects; and (iii) management improvement/projects.

The first of the targets looks at indicators like profitability, output, productivity and efficiency, while the dynamic indicators look at human resources management, corporate planning and internal programmes for employees and maintenance of equipment. The last target focuses on proper audits, financial statement, and preparation of draft PCs, procurement and general operational efficiency.

Evaluation of Performance Contracts

Evaluation of performance is the next step after target setting in performance contracts. Once the targets for a specific year are decided between the enterprise and government and the PC signed, periodic reports are prepared by the SOEs to ascertain their progress. In Ghana, these report are to be prepared on a quarterly and annual basis and sent to the SEC, which is responsible for monitoring and evaluating the reports and also prepare an annual report, which it sends to the government, based on the quarterly reports it receives from the enterprises.

The quarterly reports are prepared by the SOEs, four weeks after the end of the quarter and sent to the SEC for evaluation, and must contain the following:

i) An operating statement showing actual performance against budget for the quarter and year to date.
ii) A balance sheet as at the end of the quarter.
iii) Cash flow for the quarter showing actual against forecast.
iv) A report of capital projects compared to budget.
v) A report on the achievements of agreed performance targets.
vi) A report on progress achieved, explaining deviations and indicating the most important trends of the quarter.

The quarterly reports are the basis again for the preparation of annual reports by the SEC. This annual report prepared by the SEC is then sent to the government containing the following aspects:

i) Basic information sheet covering broad aspects of the operations of the SOEs, such as outputs, inputs, pricing and other aspects.

ii) Actual results measured against the performance targets set at the starting of the year in the PC.
iii) Performance index sheet of composite scores based on actual against target performance.
iv) Profit and loss statements.
v) Performance review assessment to ascertain reasons for departure from targets and importance of future planning.

Incentive System

The incentive forms the third essential step in implementation of performance contracts along with target setting and evaluation. Incentive can be in many forms, such as pecuniary and punitive, but in most countries pecuniary incentives in the form of bonuses are given to employees over their standard pay, as a reward for good performance. In Ghana, it is arrived at by the enterprise management, by looking at the corresponding provisions in many collective agreements for payment of an annual bonus to all employees. Hence, the employees in SOEs that perform well, can receive bonuses which are approximately 10-15 per cent of the salary of the employees.

Appraisal

An empirical study was conducted by Simpson (2013) to review the implementation of the performance contracts in Ghanaian PEs. Case studies of enterprises were used, drawn from different categories based on their performance to analyse the impact PCs had on the functioning and performance of PEs. The study broadly found that the targets and objectives of the PCs were always specific, clear and measurable. But different SOEs in different categories set different targets and objectives in their PCs.

The study divided the different parts of the PC system to analyse their implementation in SOEs. Various aspects of PCs were analysed, such as: (i) formulation of targets and objectives in PCs; (ii) institutional arrangements; (iii) resources; and (iv) politics.

Firstly, the study focuses on formulation of targets and objectives in the PCs, which the enterprises enter into; it seeks to find out if the enterprises have sufficient clarity with regard to PCs and the objectives set within them. It was found that there are significant variations in the target setting process of different SOEs in different categories. For example, the SOEs which are rated A, have very different targets on a yearly basis compared to SOEs in the remaining categories where targets are the same, except for the incremental modification to the previous years' objectives and targets. Secondly, Institutional Arrangements also differ in the different categories of SOEs in Ghana. The study finds that SOEs in categories A and B combine both a top-down and bottom-up approach while preparing the PCs, for example, SOEs in the top two categories employ a bottom-up approach while gathering information and setting of targets and objectives; however, they use a top-down approach when it comes to implementation, in the form of extensive supervision, monitoring and controlling in achieving targets. The SOEs in other categories predominantly use the top-down approach in both planning and implementation of the PCs. Thirdly, an analysis of resources is done, which, in this context, refers to the resources that are available to the SOEs to enable them to effectively implement the PCs, such as funds and other incentives. In Ghana, SOEs receive funds from various sources, such as, central government funds, Internally Generated Funds (IGF), and external sources (commercial loans and IMF/World Bank). The study finds that the resources that are available for the different categories of Ghanaian SOEs range from adequate to poor, where the SOEs in the category B have the best availability of resources. Category A enterprises also have relatively better resources, especially in the human resources area. But the resources in SOEs in the Category C and D are grossly inadequate. Lastly, the study looks at political intervention; this is an aspect that is common to most SOEs around the world and can have positive or negatives effects. The study finds that in Ghana, SOEs are significantly affected by political interventions, though the level of control differs in the different categories of SOEs. The SOEs in category B are affected by political control in the form of diverting revenues from the SOEs to other areas, while in SOEs in the categories C and D, political interference appears in the form of delays in receipts of subvention from the central government (Simpson, 2013).

The study concludes that the objectives and targets set out in the PCs in Ghanaian SOEs are always clear, specific and measurable, but different SOEs in different categories formulate these targets differently. The SOEs implement the PCs with a combination of top-down and bottom-up approaches, depending on the category in which the SOEs fall. However, all the SOEs in Ghana face similar problems with respect to availability of resources, both financial and human resources; and also face similar degrees of political control or political intervention.

Performance Contracting in China

PC plays a major role in SOEs in China, with a large number of such contracts being signed between enterprise managers and the government. Starting in the mid-1980s, the Chinese started the PC system in China and by 1986 it had acquired a significant role. The PC system had become national policy for SOE reform between 1987 and 1994. China has one of the largest experiments with performance contracting. The World Bank reports some 103,000 PCs in China in the manufacturing sector, utilities and other monopolies (Shirley and Xu, 2001).

In China, during the Cultural Revolution the remuneration for employees and managers was completely independent of individual or firm performance. In fact, the profits or losses that the firm incurred were absorbed by the state, which left managers and employees having no incentive to improve the performance of the firm. In the 1970s,this system changed and reforms started moving towards incentivising individual and enterprise performance, and so China transitioned from a centralised system where uniform wages were set by the central government, to a decentralised system where compensation for managers and workers alike, were influenced by enterprise performance, individual performance and local government policy. In the year 1978, select firms were chosen on a trial bases to try this new decentralised system where bonuses were linked to the performance of the individual; and in keeping with this policy, use of performance bonuses and piece rate began. However, the first major step came in 1979 when the Sichuan province (local government) introduced SOE contracts, where the firm's profitability was linked to the availability of performance bonuses and funds for investment (Zeitz, 2011). The SOE contracts set targets based on the previous performance of the SOEs and if the targets were met, then the SOEs were given 20 per cent of the excess over the targets, for bonuses, employee welfare and investment activities to managers and employees, thus, encouraging the managers to actively seek profits for the SOEs. SOE contracts system was also accompanied by reforms, which gave enterprise managers greater autonomy in operations, production and investment activities, so as to adapt to the new incentive system. And by early 1980s, reforms in enterprise autonomy and incentive systems were spreading far and wide in Chinese SOEs.

In China, the SOEs functioned under a rigid and cumbersome system. The management of the enterprise had no autonomy to decide on any matter. Everything was decided by the planning bodies and communicated to the managers of the SOEs; the enterprises had no claim on the profits either. The system was further complicated by the presence of a parallel management team at the top. The government and the ruling party appointed it. The contractual responsibility system introduced into the SOEs as an instrument for introducing reforms, was first started with the farm sector. The system resulted in the release of huge potential, which was unrealised for many years.

The contractual management system follows the following principles (United Nations, 1995):

i) To strengthen the enterprise and help in realising its potential.
ii) The principal of autonomy of management.
iii) The principle of responsibility binding by a contract.
iv) Rationalisation of the internal management by initiating reforms.

The system of contractual management has made clear the economic responsibility of the enterprise to the state, and has provided enterprises with relatively clearer and stable economic expectations, which have given a strong incentive to the management. The contractual system motivated by the contract incentives has promoted the reform of internal administration and thus increased the internal capacity.

Impact of Performance Contracts in Chinese SOEs

Xu and Shirley (2001) in their empirical study, analyse PCs in about 500 SOEs in China, to see the impact that PCs have had on their performance. The study categorises the contracts according to the impact the PC provisions have on the enterprises, such as:

i) Length of the contract.
ii) Wage elasticity.
iii) If the incumbent manager won the bid for the firm.
iv) If the new manager won the bid for the firm.
v) If the primary target is profit targets.
vi) If the manager posted a bond as a guarantee for performance targets.

The two main questions that the study sought to ask were: i) what impact has the PC system had on the SOEs in China?; and ii) Are the PCs important in the context of the Chinese public sector? The study concluded that the PCs did not improve productivity of SOEs overall. However, on the question of whether the PCs are important for the SOEs in China, the study says that PCs are of great importance to the public sector in China. They go on to conclude that if the PCs are designed well, keeping in mind high powered incentives, sensible targets, commitment through longer terms for managers and bonds, then they can produce positive effects. But in the absence of these, the PCs could affect the performance of the PCs. So, the study reaffirms faith in the PC system as a potential solution for improving performance of SOEs, only if done properly.

A more recent study by Zeitz (2011) identifies some of the problems with the incentive system for Chinese SOEs and their managers. The author argues that the damage caused by the performance incentive system in the long term in Chinese SOEs, outweighs the short term increase in SOE productivity. He uses empirical analysis using data from the iron and steel industry in China to analyse his hypothesis.

The Chinese government introduced the incentive system for much of the same reason that other developing countries did, that is to incentivise performance of managers and make them more accountable and to give them greater autonomy in decision-making. The incentive system in China faces several challenges: firstly,the lack of a level playing field means difficulty in implementation of the incentive system. In China, different enterprises operate differently: while some enterprises operate as protected monopolies, other SOEs are subsidised make-works for a redundant work force. The result of such diversity in the SOEs meant, that a consistent and uniform set of targets could not be set for all the SOEs. So, the government started signing enterprise specific targets and incentive system based broadly on enterprise profitability, as a performance indicator. Secondly, ownership of the SOEs was at best a contentious issue among the various levels of government, such as central government, multiple local government agencies, enterprise managers, and workers. The complexity regarding ownership also cropped up problems during the multi-party negotiations, and as a result, the local government could not formulate stable, long-term profit sharing terms with the SOEs. Finally, contracts tended to be for short periods and were fraught with pervasive negotiations; as a result, the enterprises' claims on the long term profits were in jeopardy. The managers feared that profits which would accrue from long term investment made by the SOEs, would be absorbed by the government and would not come back to the enterprise and its managers. So managers sought to make short term investment, as the benefits arising from these investments were more likely to come back to them (Zeitz, 2011).

The author concludes that the bonus system that was in place in China for SOEs between 1978 and 1988, actually had a negative impact on their performance. He attempts to contrast the short term benefits and long term effects of the incentive system, and is of the opinion that the system's negative long term effects are serious enough to justify the use of fixed wages. Policy makers are cautioned to embark on determining the long term effects of the incentive system before implementation. In the example of the iron and steel industry, the author believes that instead of the intended effect of aligning the interests of the principal and agents, the incentive system actually encourages the managers to pursue value destroying strategies.

Case Study—China: EVA as Performance Management Tool in Chinese Central SOEs

The Chinese SOEs have adopted the system of Management by Objectives (MoB). The system aims at maximisation of economic benefit and optimisation of asset efficiency. The system also aims to have fewer but better indicators. Under the system, performance assessment is done in three steps: (i) Annual Assessment & Tenure Assessment; (ii) Results Assessment and Process Evaluation; and (iii) Performance Outcomes and Incentives.

The adopted system links annual assessment results with the yearly merit pay and also links tenure assessment results with the appointment and removal, as well as, long term incentives.

The State-Owned Assets Supervision & Administration Commission of the State Council (SASAC) is the regulatory body in China, which is responsible for the SOEs. SASAC first attempted to apply the EVA system to the central Chinese SOEs in 2007 and it was out in place in 2010. The annual assessment is calculated using EVA as the major indicator, accounting for 40 per cent of the weightage. The EVA system differs from traditional financial indicators in that the EVA is the economic surplus calculated from the shareholder's (Investor's) perspective, following the shareholders' way to evaluate enterprise value. The results of adopting the EVA methodology to the performance assessment have shown positive results in the Chinese system such as:

i) A build up value of management system.
ii) Prudence in investment decision-making.
iii) Attach importance in capital management.
iv) Attach importance in research and development investment.

Presentation made by Dr Liu Yuan, Deputy Director General, Bureau of Performance Assessment, SASAC, China, at the International Workshop on Performance Evaluation and Management of State Owned Enterprises, January 2015, New Delhi.

Performance Contracting in France

The French experiment in the late 1960's was initiated with the primary objective of reducing the government's budgetary support to PEs. It was called *contract de performance* and was based on a report submitted to the French government by a committee headed by Simon Nora. It intended that there would be a mutual agreement or a contract between the government and the PEs. It was to plan the activities jointly and to establish reciprocal commitments on the part of the government and PEs (United Nations, 1995).

The French firms were facing highly competitive foreign firms and the state could not remain insensitive to the need for rationality in its budgetary decisions. The government action in the economic area had to be guided at all times by the criteria of economic efficiency. The policy of programme contracts initiated by the Nora Committee Report originated the first generation of contracts.

In the first year, only two contracts were signed, one with the French State Railways (SNCF), and other with the French State Electricity Agency (EDF). For fixing targets for price and profitability, certain indicators of efficiency were considered, like GDP, inflation rates, fuel prices, foreign exchange rates, etc. Both parties agreed that the targets could be opened for mutual discussion and further modifications. The contract was for a period of five years.

The contract provided for certain investments in growth of the PEs and the government's budgetary support for the growth was fixed. It was agreed that prices of the goods and the services produced by PEs could be adjusted without prior government approval, to cover variable costs and two thirds of the financial needs on the new investment (Jhon, 1988).

The contracts proceeded well during the initial years but with the oil crisis in 1973, most of the macroeconomic assumptions were thrown overboard, and the government went back on the agreement. It did not allow companies to increase the prices, as per the contract. The EDF contract was not renewed, while that of the Railways was renewed for only two years.

It was again the report of *de la Geniere* in 1977 which was the starting point for the contracts of the second generation—the *Contracts de Enterprise* or the Enterprise Contracts. While the basic approach of this report was similar to that of the Nora Committee Report, it strongly advocated the preparation of long term plans for each enterprise, which would form the basis for the contracts.

The second round of contracts was initiated in 1978-79 with four enterprises namely SNCF, Coal Company, General Maritime and Air France. The duration was reduced to three years. It was to ensure better appreciation of the economic environment that might affect enterprise operations. But in 1981, when the Socialist party came to power, these contracts were subjected to rough weather. Only the contract with Air France was operational because it was in a globally competitive environment. These experiences dampened the spirits of French enthusiasm for performance contracts.

In the French experiment, the institutional arrangements were quite simple. The administrative machinery monitoring the PE included the formation of a committee. It included all other ministries involved in the activities of the PE. Another was also formed of the board of directors who would constantly monitor negotiations, with the CEO as the chief negotiating agent. There was a constant flow of information between the board of the directors, the CEO, other executives and the workers. Due to the information asymmetry between the government and the enterprise, there were long delays in negotiations and some of the contracts took years to negotiate and finalise (Carsalade, 1986). In addition, the French system did not introduce any special rewards for achieving the targets and penalties for non-fulfillment of the terms of the contract.

Institutional Arrangements

In France, no separate institutional arrangements were set up for the formulation of the *Contact de Programme*. The French thought that it would be adequate for one committee to be set up, representing the government and negotiating the contract with the PE. The administrative ministry was to preside over the committee. Several other ministries, such as ministry of Foreign Trade, Ministry of Vocational Education, Ministry of Solidarity, were also to be on the committee. It was realised that if all the ministries affected by the performance of public entetprises were to be included the negotiations would take a lot of time. This difficulty was overcome by arranging a committee with representatives from only the nodal ministry, which sets the policies for the particular sector in question, and representatives of the Ministry of State Planning, Ministry of Economy, dealing with Finance and External Affairs.

On the PEs side, it was provided that the CEO should negotiate the contract, and report to the director of the company. Constant flow of information between the board of directors and through the board to the executives and workers was deemed necessary (Sharma, 1982).

Appraisal

The problems that had come up with the French contracts were that they were subjective in nature and did not clearly specify the targets. There were many reasons for this lack of clarity. Often in addition to goals regarding financial and physical productivity, several qualitative and intrinsically un-measurable objectives were specified in the contracts. As a result, a manager would not know how to prioritise between conflicting objectives. Neither the evaluator would know weather to reward or punish the manager for a situation, when the object is over achieved or under achieved.

A shortcoming of the French system was that it did not provide for any correction of the information asymmetry between the government and the enterprise. The French government was totally dependent on the enterprises for information and for setting the targets. This led to long delays in negotiating contracts, and specifying the targets in conditional terms. This conditionality led to frequent renegotiating of the contracts. Much of this could have been averted if there had been a PIS.

The Signaling System

The system adopted by Pakistan, Korea, and Venezuela for improving PEP (public enterprise performance) is referred to as the Signaling System. Contracts between the PE and the government are just one part of this system. The main objective of the system is to send signals to the managers to guide them in making decisions in the national interest and to reward them for doing so.

The theoretical foundations of this system are more solid, because in the development of this system, the previous experience with performance evaluation in developing countries was carefully considered. Briefly, the Signaling System consists of three-sub systems (Istaqbal, 1985):

i) Performance Information System (PIS).

ii) Performance Evaluation System.

iii) Performance Incentive System.

In order to negotiate appropriate targets and monitor enterprise performance, it is essential that there should be a reasonable balance of information between the government and the PE. The purpose of a PIS is to ensure this balance. It is different from the MIS (Management Information System).

In all the three countries that adopted the Signaling System, the development of a computerised PIS was considered a necessary precondition. Accordingly, software titled Public Enterprise Performance Information System (PEPIS) was developed. This software was initially developed for Pakistan and subsequently adopted for Korea and Venezuela.

The PES consists of several steps. Firstly, one has to decide on a set of appropriate criteria for evaluating enterprise performance. The signaling system tries to measure performance on four fronts (Istaqbal, 1985):

i) Static Efficiency: Is the firm making the best use of its given stock of resources?

ii) Dynamic Efficiency: Many decisions made by an enterprise have costs (benefits) in the present but generate benefits (costs) in the future. Therefore, it is important to ensure that the enterprise is making optimum decisions in the dynamic sense also. This involves answering questions like, is preventive maintenance adequate? Is the company devoting enough attention to Research and Development?

iii) Project Implementation: Are the projects being implemented efficiently?

iv) Achievement of non-commercial objectives: A system has to be devised to measure the efforts of the enterprise on this front.

The Pakistani Experience

Signaling System was established essentially in Pakistan to improve the operational efficiency of Public Industrial Enterprises. Until the late 1970s, these enterprises were characterised by a combination of adverse financial and operational features, they were under severe declining profitability, leading to weak financial structures. They developed imbalances in debt equity ratios and inefficient assets usage, etc. As a result, in the early 1980s, the government entrusted the task of new investments to the private sector. The public sector was expected to improve its operational efficiency. The Government of Pakistan took a decision to adopt the Signaling System for improving the efficiency of the PEs.

During 1981, in order to improve the efficiency of the Public Industrial Sector under the Ministry of Production, the Government decided to set up the Signaling System. In November 1981, the Experts Advisory Cell (EAC) was given the responsibility of setting up the project. The project had three components (Shaikh, 1986):

i) A PIS to measure accurately actual behaviour.

ii) A PES to specify socially desirable behaviour.

iii) A Performance Incentive System to reward or penalise managers for their actual performance at the end of the period, i.e., one year.

The development of the system took about three years. During this process, major efforts were made to evolve a PIS. In 1983, the government approved the operation of the system with modifications. The Signaling System originally envisaged social profitability, known as public profitability, as the primary indicator of performance. However, in approving the Signaling System, private profitability instead of proposed public profitability at constant prices, was kept as the primary criterion of evaluation.

Thus, two thirds of the system, i.e., the PIS and Performance Incentive System survived. The third part suffered a major conceptual blow. According to Shaikh (1986), the real reasons for this conceptual compromise were as follows:

i) The government feared situations in which loss-making firms may have to be given a bonus because they performed well in terms of public profitability at constant prices.

ii) It was deemed that the public relations and political costs associated with such cases might be too heavy.

iii) Further, the government thought that by opting for financial profits as target, it would be able to deal more effectively with the constant nuisance of petitions for relief by loss-making enterprises.

Following this policy as the first step, several re-organisational measures were adopted to streamline the public sector. At the completion of this exercise, a fairly smooth control structure emerged. In this organisational set up, the ministry was operating like the head office of a large industrial conglomerate, the Experts Advisory Cell (EAC), an independent technical unit, was created to assist the ministry in performing this function. The need for this unit was felt, since the ministry run by the civil servants was not equipped with the expertise required for the new function. One of the first tasks of the cell was to identify the ways and means of improving the performance of PEs. It was identified that there was a need for setting up institutional arrangements to guide and evaluate the performance of managers, so that they could also be rewarded for good performance. It was against this background that the signaling project was developed at EAC. The principles on which the EAC in Pakistan sets the targets are (Istaqbal, 1985):

i) Efficient targets setting should be carried out in a participatory process; without this approach targets tend to take the form of formal derivatives, which are often overtly accepted and covertly resisted.

ii) Targets should be clear-cut.

iii) Targets should neither be too low or too high.

iv) Each enterprise must be looked at in its own unique environment, which must be taken into account.

v) The targets for incentives should ensure that the generation of a surplus is significantly more than distribution, by way of bonus.

vi) Targets must take into account the social tasks, which enterprises are invariably asked to carry out.

Appraisal

The Signaling System was introduced in Pakistan in 1983-84. Since then, a number of studies have been carried out to determine the impact of the system on enterprise performance. The World Bank undertook a comprehensive study (Shirley, 1988), covering 12 enterprises and analysed their performance for the period 1983-1986. It was based on the quantitative measures as well as qualitative evidence. The study tried to answer two issues:

i) did the system succeeded in achieving its stated objectives of improving private financial profit and
ii) did it result in any efficiency gain, which was an underlying assumption of the system.

The study found it impossible to establish a link between the performance changes and the Signaling System. The factors examined were pricing, macroeconomic changes in management and changes in the market. Out of the four factors, pricing policy was the only one that definitely affected the extent to which achieving private profit targets. Efficiency trends in public profit did not show a strong correlation with growth in GDP, thus indicating that macroeconomic changes perhaps did not have a strong bearing on enterprise performance. Similarly increased competition was not a major factor explaining the improvements in efficiency, but it was a reason for the deterioration in results in some cases. Lastly, changes in management did bring about some efficiency gain. The changes were caused by a variety of reasons in which the Signaling System played an important role.

A later study, which also combined quantitative and qualitative methods to identify the impact of the Signaling System on the SOEs performance, came to the conclusion that the system in Pakistan at best, has been a qualified success. The expectations that the system gave birth to, at the time of its initiation, have remained unfulfilled to a great extent It highlighted that, to a large extent, the government failed to appreciate the full potential of the system, which resulted in a unhappy outcome. It was felt that the system had the capacity to increase productivity gains, to which the government paid very little attention. The government did not make any attempt to use the large volume of information thrown up by the system, to review the macroeconomic policy framework. The study concluded that, "the logical consequence of this seeming apathy is that the system has been reduced to routine reporting exercise."

The African Experience

Though quite a few LDCs may claim to have had a contractual relationship between their government and PE, the credit for pioneering this system goes to Senegal. They were the first LDC's to adopt the French model. Since the French government advisors set up the process, the Senegalese contract system turned out to be very similar to that of the French contracts. The initiative for adopting this system came from the Prime Minister's Office (PMO). The PE managers welcomed it. They looked at it as an opportunity to get compensated for the non-commercial objectives imposed on them. Through it, they also hoped for increased autonomy and decreased outside interference. The technical and financial ministries, on the other hand, resented the curb on their powers and were not as enthusiastic.

The Senegalese contracts, as already mentioned, bear a remarkable similarity to the French contracts. The PMO was involved in the design and execution of the contracts. The contracts did not work the way they should have. It was primarily because preconditions relating to criteria were not satisfactorily fulfilled. The Senegalese contracts had terminology like "accommodate", "obligation", which were vague and made the whole exercise very subjective. The heavy emphasis, according to a World Bank report (Shirley, 1983) was on the fact that,performance of virtually all enterprises in the sector began to show a dramatic deterioration in the contract periods. This result was a direct consequence of the way contracts were structured. The entire exercise had a positive influence too. The PEs started strategic planning for the first time. The government started seriously comparing the costs of social objectives and investment proposals with their benefits.

Performance Contracts in Gambia

The PCS for PEs was introduced in Gambia in 1987. As a prelude to identifying those PEs to come under the PCS, the PE sector was divided into three schedules (United Nations, 1995):

i) Enterprises in which the government is a minority shareholder.

ii) Enterprises in which the government is a majority shareholder.

ii) Strategic corporations/departments.

In 1987, under the first phase, PCs were developed for three enterprises only. Under the second phase in 1990, performance contracts were developed for another three enterprises. In 1994, the third phase included another three enterprises.

The contracts were executed for a period of three years, and were signed by his Excellency, the President, on behalf of the government, and by the managing director on behalf of the enterprise. The PC followed the following steps:

i) Definition of the enterprise.

ii) Identification of the commercial and non-commercial activities of the enterprise.

iii) Development of the mechanism for reimbursement of non-commercial/social services.

iv) Selection of performance indicators and fixing targets for a particular year.

v) Determination of management incentive/sanctions scheme.

Institutional Arrangements

After the introduction of the PCS, the ultimate control and responsibility was taken over by the Office of the President. The President executed the contracts on behalf of the government. The steering committees had representatives from the line ministries, the Office of the President, National Investment Boards (NIB) and the enterprises themselves. These committees were given the responsibility of approving the budgets, deciding upon the performance indicators, targets, performance evaluation and management incentive (bonus)/ sanctions. The line ministries were expected to concentrate their efforts on the development of sectoral policies, objectives and the framework within which PEs were expected to operate.

The following infrastructure arrangements were made for implementing the contract:

i) For each enterprise, a Steering Committee was set up comprising, the Chief Executive of NIB, Secretary General of the Office of the President, permanent secretaries of the ministries of finance, economic affairs, trade and industry and the line ministry, and the Solicitor General.

ii) NIB reviews the Corporate plan, annual budget, performance indicators, targets, weights, and cost of non-commercial activities in the coming year.

iii) Members of the Steering Committee also review the corporate plan, annual budget, and performance indicators, targets and weights, along with the NIB comments, and agree on the contracts.

iv) Contracts are signed by the president on behalf of the government and by the managing director on behalf of the enterprise.

v) The enterprise submits quarterly and annual performance reports.

vi) NIB receives the annual audited accounts and management's self-assessment of performance, and makes an evaluation and a recommendation on the bonus to be paid, or penalty to be applied.

vii) Office of the President reviews and approves the evaluation and award of bonus or application of penalty.

viii) Bonus is paid to management and distributed at their discretion.

Results

The Gambian system is generally counted as successful in achieving a sustained improvement in the performance of PEs. The system had commitment at the highest level with the president being a part of the coritract signing process. The contracts were based on the Corporate Plan, which strengthened the enterprises information system further.

The system also had a well-developed Incentive System, which boosted the working of the contracts. According to a study conducted by Pervaiz, the Gambian Ports Authority (GPA) significantly improved its performance. The net profits on port operations increased from 6.6 million in 1986-87 to 28.2 million in 1992-93. Gambia Produce Marketing Board showed substantial improvements after signing the contracts. Gambian Telecom Company too significantly improved its net profits after the contract.

The Experience in Bangladesh

Bangladesh initiated the process of contracting in the year 1985. Only those enterprises, which belonged to the category 'A', i.e., only those enterprises, which generated exceptionally good revenue, 89 per cent of the total revenue, are included in the category of contract signing enterprises.

The process of contracting in Bangladesh begins with preparing the performance improvement plan. Analysis of the objectives of the enterprise as well as the past performance of the enterprise is observed in order to formulate a true picture. This is followed by identification of critical success factors and classifying the factor of accountability. This leads to a discussion of strategic issues of the enterprise, which culminates into the formulation of a performance improvement plan.

The next step of the process involves defining the performance criteria and assigning weightages to them. A process of negotiating the targets with the concerned ministries and committees and finalising the draft follows this. The next steps is monitoring the contracts, both quarterly and bimonthly, through a monitoring system and take necessary corrective action if necessary.

A typical PC of an enterprise would include (United Nations, 1995): (i) production, (ii) profitability, (iii) FIRD, and (iv) International Management Systems.

Institutional Arrangements

The institutional arrangement supporting the implementation of the contracts comprise a Council Committee on Public Enterprise, Chaired by the president, and a Secretary's Committee on Public

Enterprises, convened by the Ministry of Finance. These are supported by an ad-hoc Task Force, which comprises of experts of different areas of public sector. The Council Committee on Public Enterprises manages issues pertaining to the public sector, reviews the contracts, gives guidelines, examines, evaluates the reports and initiates corrective action. And the Secretaries Committee consists of secretaries of ministries divisions of 'A' category of enterprises; secretary PEs; secretary planning commission; secretary finance.

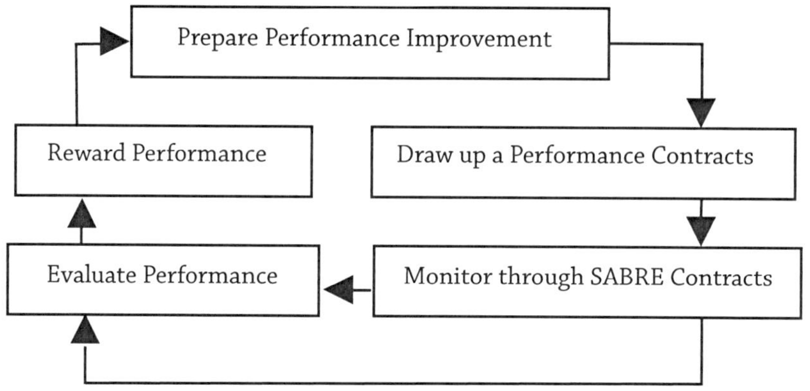

Performance Contracting Cycle

The Sri Lankan Experience

Sri Lanka experimented with the PCS only for a very brief period. In 1991 two enterprises, namely Sri Lanka Tyre Corporation and Ceylon weather Products Corporation, were selected for the purpose. However with the privatisation of both the enterprises in 1993, the system was not tried out in other enterprises.

Sri Lanka adopted the signaling system for designing the PCfor the two enterprises. The performance contracts focussed on financial performance (90% in the case of Sri Lanka Tyre and 97 per cent in respect of Ceylon Leather) and very little attention was paid to dynamic factors. Human resource development was the only dynamic performance criteria included in the PCS. It is quite possible that the designs of the performance contracts were influenced by the ultimate objective of privatisation.

A study done by Dheerasesera and Knight-John (Mohnot, 1997) says that the failure of PCS in Sri Lanka was due to the lack of political commitment.

Performance contracting should not be viewed as an alternative or competition to privatisation. The study brings out the fact that the Sri Lankan government was not able to pursue the policy of gradual divestment because it was under pressure from the donor institutions to complete the privatisation programme and this was the cause for the failure.

The Experience of Thailand

Thailand is the latest entrant in the performance contracting community. The Thai cabinet approved the introduction of the system in June 1995. The performance agreement system introduced in Thailand is similar to the Signaling System. The evaluation is done on a five-point scale. The cabinet also approved an incentive scheme based on performance. The Office of Auditor General is responsible for administering and implementing the system. The performance contracting system was applied to 53 enterprises in 1998.

Summing Up

Performance contracting for PEs has been a process initiated by the European countries, especially with France taking the initiative. The system has been duplicated in many countries. They have been adopted as it is, in many of them, while a few countries have modified them according to their conditions. The system has done not as well as it was expected to do at the time of initiation. A number of factors can be identified for the system not being very successful. The other important features of the system like infrastructure support, contents, duration, are taken up in the coming chapters.

Case Study: Bhutan—Performance Compacts

In 2007, the Bhutanese Royal Government, through a royal charter, established Druk Holdings and Investments (DHI) to hold and manage the existing and future investments of the Royal Government for the long term benefit of the citizens of Bhutan. The company holds 18 different companies with varying control interest. The Ministry of Finance is the sole shareholder with regards to Druk Holdings and Investment.

The company has in place, a performance management system in the form of annual performance compacts. The compacts permeate various levels from the Ministry of Finance and DHI all the way to the employees of companies, such as, a compact between the Ministry of Finance and DHI, DHI Board and DHI compact, DHI and companies compact, companies and department/division compacts, departments and employees compacts.

The annual compact cycle starts with the planning and setting of targets. The first step in this is to identify the activities linked to the outcomes and outputs, followed by the setting of annual targets and the finalising the draft compact. The next stage of the compact cycle includes monitoring and coaching, where the mid-term compact deliverables are submitted and mid-term reviews are conducted. The third stage is the evaluation of performance where the annual compact deliverables are submitted and annual compact evaluation is conducted, and finally the last step of the annual cycle ends with the recognition and awarding performance incentives.

The document is structured in two sections. The first section elaborates the performance indicators, which are of two kinds: financial and non-financial indicators. The second section of the compact details each of the financial and non-financial indicators. The document has four columns where the first column lists out the performance indicators, which are divided into financial compacts which have 50 per cent weightage and non-financial indicators make up the other 50 per cent of the weightage. The second column assigns target outputs for the performance indicators listed out in the second column, and third column sets deadlines for the achievement of the targets and target outputs and the last column of the document allots the weightage to each of the targets and indicators for the performance evaluation.

The institutional mechanisms for the performance evaluation include the CPD, DHI which is responsible for the planning, monitoring and evaluation of the performance compacts; while the Board Committee for Performance Management (BCPM) is responsible for the recognition and performance incentive, which are to be given at the end of the annual cycle of the compacts. The performance incentives for the company are based on a Compact Achievement Points (CAP).

The table below explains the PBVA awarded for different achievement levels of the compact.

Compact Achievement Points (CAP)	PBVA Paid
CAP<= 75%	No PBVA paid
CAP>= 95%	Full PBVA paid (25% of 12 months pay for CEO and 10% for other employees)
If 75%<CAP<= 95%	Prorated -1.25% PBVA for every % point of achievement and 0.5% for other employees

Presentation made by Dr Damber S. Kharkha, Director, Corporate Performance Department, Druk Holdings and Investment (DHI), Bhutan, at the International Workshop on Performance Evaluation and Management of State Owned Enterprises, January 2015, New Delhi.

References

Adda, W.A. (1994). *Performance Contracts in Ghana.* A case study prepared for Commonwealth Secretariat. London. p.I.

Cadic, Jean-Yves (1979). *The Program Contract: An Attempt to Rationalize the Management of Public Enterprises.* Doctrine. 20 December.

Carsalade, Yves (1986). "PE, State Plan and Managerial Autonomy: The French Experience", in S.B. Jam (ed.), Management and Role of PE: Indo-French Experience. Vol. 1. Published by BPE, India in collaboration with SCOPE. Delhi.

Istaqbal, Mehdi (1985). *Setting Targets for Improving Costs Efficiencies in Public Enterprises: A Study of Pakistan.* Presented in a seminar at Karachi. July.

Jhon, Nellis (1988). "Contract Plans and Public Enterprise Performance", *Working Papers Country Economics Department.* Washington, DC: The World Bank.

Kim, Kwanbo and Pan S. Kim (2001). "Restructuring, Management Innovation, and Privatisation of State-Owned Enterprises in South Korea", in Korean Social Science Journal 28(2): 67. Singapur: Springer Internat.

Mohnot, S.R. (1997). "Basic Issues in Performance Contracting with Special Reference to Indian Case", Paper presented at the International Conference on Performance Contracting. New Delhi. 13-15 January.

Park, Young C. (1986). "A System for Evaluating the Performance of Government Invested Enterprises in the Republic of Korea", in Prajapati Trivedi (ed.) (1990), *Memorandum of Understanding: An Approach to Improving Public Enterprise Performance.* New Delhi: International Management Publishers. p.523.

Sharma, Shreedhar (1982). "The Enterprise Contract System in Public Enterprise Management", *IPE Journal*, December.

Shaikh, Abdul Hafeez (1986). *Performance Evaluation of Public Enterprises: Lessons from the Pakistan Experience.* Paper presented at AIES, New Orleans. December.

Shirley, Mary (1983). "Contracts between the States and its Public Enterrpises: The Experience of France and Senegal", *World Bank discussion paper* no 577.

Shirley, Mary (1988). "Public Enterprises Performance Evaluation System in Pakistan", *World Bank discussion paper.* November.

Shirley, Mary M. and Lixin Colin Xu (2001). "Empirical Effects of Performance Contracts: Evidence from China", Journal of Law, Economics & Organisation 17(1): 168-200 (April).

Simpson, Samuel Nana Yaw (2013). "Performance Contract and Performance of Public Enterprises: A Study of the Implementation Processes", *Journal of Public Administration and Governance* 3(2): 16..

Song, Dae-Hee (1988) "New Public Enterprise Policy and Efficiency Improvement", in Prajapati Trivedi (ed.) (1990), *Memorandum of Understanding: An Approach to Improving Public Enterprise Performance.* New Delhi: International Management Publishers. pp. 581.

Trivedi, Prajapathi (1968). "Theory and Practice of the French System of Contracts for Improving Public Enterprise Performance", *ICPE Journal* 8(1): 28 41.

United Nations (1995). *A Handbook for Performance Contracting in Public Enterprises.* New York: Department of Development and Management Services.

Zeitz, Peter (2011). *Short-Run Incentives and Myopic Behavior: Evidence from State-Owned Enterprises in China.*

Annexure Table A-1.1

Contracting System in France, Korea, and India

Name	*Policy*	*Contents of the Contract*	*Institutional Arrangements*	*Special Features*
France	Nora Committee recommendation for setting up of a performance contracting system for improving the PE performance.	1) Corp plan. 2) Stategy adopted by the enterprise. 3) Areas of financial relation with the government. 4) Government obligations.	1) A committee representing the Govt. 2) Representation from the PE.	Highly obejective assessment
Korea	The GIE Act. 1983, empowering GIE's more autonomy and powers.	Qualitative Indicators 1) Public Profitability 2) Reserves 3) Intermediate Cost sales 4) R & D Expenditure quantitative Indicators 1) Corp Planning 2) R&D 3) MIS 4) Service Quality	1) MEC 2) Ad-hoc task Force 3) PE bureau	Political commitment at the highest level
India	1985 Arjun Sengupta Committee Recommendtions	Financial Indicators 1) Profits 2) sales 3) Turnover Non Financial Indicators 1) HRD 2) MoU submission 3) Energy 4) Environment 5) Project Imp	1) HPC 2) Ad-hoc Task Force 3) PE bureau	1) Absence of commitment at the political level 2) Minimum flow of information between the signatories.

Source: PhD thesis submitted by Potaraju, 2000.

2

Evolution and Growth of MoU System in India

In this chapter, we look at the MoU system in India. In particular, we will focus on the evolution of the system from its genesis to present day, and the need for MoUs in the context of CPSEs in India. Some important questions regarding the functioning of the system in India will be examined, such as, why was a need felt to introduce the MoU system in India, how has the MoU document changed over the decades and what are the different factors which warranted changes in the MoU document? The answer to these questions will enable us to gain a comprehensive and holistic understanding of the MoU system.

As to the question of why the system was needed in India, we would have to first look at the role of PEs (Public Enterprises) in India and understand the evolution of the public sector. Secondly, expectations from the PEs and the reality of the PEs, in the context of the Indian economy will be examined. The MoU system endeavors to provide a level playing field for both the enterprise managers, and ministries, to negotiate performance targets. There are also other problems like information asymmetry, that the MoU system seeks to counteract. We will look at landmark committee reports to analyse the evolution of the MoU system in India.

Arjun Sengupta Report

The origins of the MoU system can be found in the Arjun Sengupta Committee Report,[1] which, as early as 1984, explored the possibility of introducing an MoU between the administrative ministry and the PE managers. The MoU was to be the critical interface in the relationship between the ministry and the public sector, which was ambiguous until then. The main drive of the report, however, was not the introduction of the MoU system but was rather the state of affairs in the public sector and the challenges it faced. The report goes on to

1. Arjun Sengupta Committee Report, 1984

detail the functioning and role of public sector in India at the time, and also talks about the theoretical foundations of the public sector in India.

Foundations of the Public Sector

The beginnings of the public sector in India can be found in the Industrial Policy Resolution of 1956. These were the formative years of our nation, and government at the time introduced this policy to address two important aspects, namely: a socialistic society and the need for planned and rapid development. In order to achieve this, the government declared that all the sectors, i.e. basic, strategic and public utility, must be in the public sector. In the following decades, PEs occupied the commanding heights of the economy and set the course, in large part, for development in the country. The committee says, that as a result, the public sector enterprises had become the primary tool for planning in the country.

Another important step in shaping the development of public sector in India, is the Second Five Year Plan, which spells out the critical link between planning and growth of the public sector, and highlights the importance of three main components when using modern technology, namely: (i) large scale production, (ii) unified control, and (iii) allocation of resources on certain main-lines of activity.

Role and Importance of the Public Sector in India

The Industrial Policy Resolution of 1956 met with great success. PEs dominated the Schedule 'A' industries—core sectors such as coal, heavy engineering, steel, non-ferrous metals etc., and also managed to have substantial presence in Schedule 'B' industries—machine tools, fertilisers, basic and intermediate chemicals and drugs, etc. The size of the public sector grew from a mere 5 PEs in 1951 to 209 in 1983, indicating the incredible success and proliferation of the public sector in India. The report says that in 1983-84, capital employed in the CPSEs (central public sector enterprises) alone stood at ₹32,202 crore with a turnover of ₹46,777 crores. The committee also identified the important achievements of the public sector in the context of the Indian economy:

i) Production in terms of quantitative targets was boosted in the country through PEs.
ii) The foundations of the modern industrial base were established by the PEs.
iii) Public sector was responsible for a more balanced regional development around the country.
iv) Development of technological skills and know how proliferated through the industry.

Yet, the committee believed that for all the contributions and achievements of the public sector to the Indian economy and Indian manufacturing, the overall performance of the various PEs (public enterprises) remained unsatisfactory and failed to fulfil some of its main objectives namely, generation of resources and financial profitability. The public sector was expected to generate resources through manufacturing and other activities to further establish more industries, the PEs were not fulfiling this to the expected level. Financially, the public sector was expected to be a significant source of revenue for the state, revenue, which would in turn be used by the government for further development of fresh fields, which it did not fulfil.

Expectations from the Public Sector

The Industrial Policy Resolution of 1956 was clear in setting out three essential questions regarding the public sector namely:
i) Why the state was operating PEs.
ii) What was expected from the PEs in the context of the Indian economy, and
iii) How they were to operate in order to meet the expectation of the State.

The resolution sets out that with the increasing importance of public sector and the participation of the government in the economy some essential policy have to be adopted, namely:[2]
i) Necessity to take speedy decisions and assume responsibility in order for PEs to be successful.

2. Ibid.: 19.

ii) Authority must be decentralised and management of PEs must be along the line of a business or a private company.

iii) It was expected that the public sector would augment the revenue of the state and contribute to resource generation for further development in fresh fields and sectors.

iv) Even if some of the enterprises incur losses, the performance of the PEs must be judged by their total results.

v) And finally, PEs must have the largest possible measure of freedom in their functioning and operations.

The public sector however, did not perform as expected in terms of the abovementioned objectives. One of the expectations from the public sector enterprises was that they would operate on the lines of a business and generate revenue which could be further invested in growth and development. The PEs were not successful as commercial ventures and so could not augment the revenue stream of the government. Efficiency in operation was another expectation that was not fulfiled by the PEs where both commercial and non-commercial enterprises saw a deterioration of efficiency. The resolution also envisages the greatest measure of freedom to the PEs in their operation, however, this freedom was curtailed in a lot of cases or there was interference from the government in an unofficial manner. Lastly, the evaluation systems developed by the government to monitor the performance of the PEs were not successful in judging the overall results of the PEs.[3]

The public sector on almost all counts did not perform as expected, be it profitability or productivity as set out by the resolution of 1956 and was in need of reform to tackle the challenges facing it and some of the solutions set out by the committee are set out below.

Accountability

The Arjun Sengupta Committee report identified several area of concern in terms of the functioning and operation of the public sector in view of the failure of the PEs in meeting the expectation set forth in the Industrial Policy Resolution and Second Five Year

3. Ibid.: 19.

Plan. One the measures suggested was the possible introduction of the Memorandum of Understanding as a measure of accountability of the PEs and the encourage them to function more along the lines of a commercial venture.

The problem areas identified by the report which needs to be addressed are:

i) Organisational structures in PEs.
ii) Autonomy in PEs.
iii) Accountability of enterprises.
iv) Technological upgradation.
v) Financial viability of loss making units: capital restructuring and closure.
vi) Pricing in PEs.
vii) Other issues.

With the idea of increasing the accountability of the PEs for their performance an evaluation system was suggested by the committee in the form of the MoU. This MoU was to be signed between the enterprise managers and the administrative ministry concerned before the commencement of the financial year. The committee earmarks 4 specific categories of criteria and select indicators for measuring the performance of the PEs. The four categories are:[4]

Financial Performance

Financial performance is regarded as the most important criteria as the report believes that in order for PEs to mobilise resources they have to necessarily be financially viable and the indicators suggested are:

i) gross margin on assets (for all enterprises);
ii) net profit on net worth (for core and profit making enterprises);
iii) gross margin on sales (for service enterprises).

The criteria and indicators that are applicable to PEs are supposed to depend on the type of industry the PE belongs to and profitability of the enterprise.

4. Ibid.: 29.

Productivity and Cost Reduction

This category of criteria supplements the monitoring of financial performance by using simple indicators to monitor productivity and costs. The indicators suggested are:

i) Capacity utilisation.

ii) Raw material costs (at constant prices) per unit of output.

iii) Value added per rupee of wages.

The committee recommends that an overall index be prepared of the cost of production, whenever possible.

Technical Dynamism

This group of criteria relate to development of technology in the form of product or process innovations and patents relating to the same. This category of indicators is a little more difficult to define in quantitative indicators. So, in addition to the number of patents obtained for the above mentioned innovations the following are indicators used to measure technical dynamism of a PE:

i) Reduction of cost of production as a percentage of its total cost.

ii) Efficiency level of the product.

iii) Export competitiveness.

iv) Sale of know-how.

Project Implementation

At the time, there was already a system of reporting progress of the projects, which the committee believed was too cumbersome to provide a simple measure of quality of performance with regards to project implementation and goes on to suggest the following indicators which could be used:

i) Percentage utilisation of plan funds.

ii) Average slippage in ongoing projects, the weights for the average being defined by the cost of each project.

iii) Percentage cost revision for the approved investment programme relative to the previous year.

Recommendation Regarding MoU Process

The PES (performance evaluation system) suggested by the Arjun Sengupta Committee makes use of roughly 10 or so indicators for enterprises operating in core sectors and a significantly smaller number of indicators in the case of non-core sectors. It is recommended that there be a quarterly reporting of the status of the indicators by the enterprises. The committee goes on suggest an annual performance evaluation report which is to be prepared by the administrative ministry along with representatives from the Planning Commission and BPE which should be available before the annual plan discussion as the committee believes that unless the performance evaluation is taken into account in the process of investment decisions, appointments, confirmations, promotions and extensions for top management, it will lack the bite that it needs in order to be an effective tool for measuring performance.

The committee also recommends that the then existing system of MIS (Management Information System) be abandoned as the PES that is suggested by the committee is a much simpler alternative. The government must insist that in each public sector unit there should be a well defined MIS linking all costs and profit centers to the top and that the MIS should be the basis for reporting performance indicators to the government, so that they are always in a position to provide clarification to the government when needed. And lastly, the committee suggested indicators which would become the basis for top management to monitor a wide range of production, productivity and cost variable and in doing so would bring about improvement in efficiency and profitability.

Study on the Revamping of the MoU System, NCAER

A study was conducted in 2004, by the National Council of Applied Economic Research (NCAER, 2004). The study is the basis of major changes in the MoU system post 2004. For the first time importance was given to productivity in PSEs and not just the financial aspects alone. Greater weightage was assigned to dynamic factors like quality, R&D and customer satisfaction as a measure of the performance of the PSEs. Focus was laid on the functioning of the MoU system in India and more specifically, on the challenges faced in the implementation of the system. The study uses various methods to assess and evaluate the effectiveness of the MoU system and makes suitable recommendations for its improvement. Several important concepts such as the use of TFP (total factor productivity) analysis as a composite measure of the effectiveness of the MoU system were incorporated. Inputs were taken from enterprise managers from select CPSEs to gauge the perception of the MoU system among CPSEs.

The study attempts to identify the problems faced by the public sector in India. The study, while reiterating the role of the public sector played in India as discussed in the Arjun Sengupta Committee report and identifies the serious problems which hindered the performance of the public sector enterprises. The following are some of the problems identifies by the NCAER study (2004: 2):

i) Dysfunctional relationship between the PSEs and government.
ii) General lack of clarity as to what was expected from enterprises.
iii) Multiplicity of goals leading to confusion among managers with regard to profit objectives.
iv) Lack of proper methods of accountability and evaluation.

Government interference in operations of the CPSEs was prevalent as the enterprises were regarded as subordinate departments rather than corporate bodies, which led to a dysfunctional relationship between the government and enterprises. The public sector in developing countries were set up with both a social function and a profit motive, managers did not have clear directions or guidelines as to what function was to take precedence causing a lack of clarity as to the expectations from enterprises. The abovementioned problem was supplemented by multiple goals that the CPSEs are expected to meet some of which were mutually contradictory. And finally, the government was not adequately equipped to understand the finer nuances of the operation of the enterprises. All the information and expertise was with the managers in the enterprises and so the government did not have the tools or the expertise to evaluate the performance of the CPSEs and hold them accountable. The study says that it is against this background that the need for the MoU system was felt.

What is Memorandum of Understanding?

MoU system was first introduced in its test phase in 1987-88 based on the French system of performance contracting and a year later it switched to the signaling system which is still followed. The system was introduced on the concept of MBO (management by objectives) to give greater autonomy to managers in the public sector and simultaneously make them more accountable for the performance of the enterprises. In its most basic form, the MoU system is a system of management audit (NCAER, 2004: 2). In light of the inefficiencies that crept into many enterprises and the need to accurately evaluate the performance of the CPSEs the MoU system was introduced to evaluate the performance of the public sector enterprises as against select goals and objectives set for them every year.

Further, the study espouses another important function of the MoU system which is to address the problem of information asymmetry between the managers and the government. The managers of the enterprises at any given point have more information regarding the operation of the enterprise, be it financial information or technical information. The enterprises could use this advantage to pursue their own interests which are at contradictory to the interests of the government.

The study also says that the document itself has changed unrecognisably since it was introduced in its original form in the mid-1980s. The focus moved to bring about a more holistic growth in the enterprises as opposed to only financial growth, and as a result dynamic indicators like HRD (human resource development), R&D (research and development) and customer management were accorded greater importance in the context of the MoU system, thus, incentivising both long term and short term growth. At the time of the study the MoU document had a healthy mixture of financial, dynamic and efficiency indicators. Reflecting the shift in attitude regarding how the PSEs were viewed. They were to operate in the free markets and as such had to develop their own revenue and not depend on the government for their basic operations.

Perception of MoU in PSEs

The NCAER study got feedback from enterprise managers and CEOs regarding certain key questions about the functioning of the MoU system. A total of 33 select enterprises were chosen and detailed questionnaires were sent. Some of the areas that the study focused on for feedback were (NCAER, 2004: 7): (i) role and relevance of the MoU system; (ii) output; (iii) outcome; and (iv) path forward.

At the outset, the study believes that the MoU system was still relevant as of 2004-05. However, it goes on to say that the system had imperfections and needed change. From the responses it received from enterprises the study confirms the importance of the MoU document to the PSEs and their managers, in fact, the study says that the perception among enterprise managers is that the MoU system was critical and instrumental in improving standards like productivity and helped in effective utilisation of latent infrastructure, social, physical and financial. According to the PSEs "governance along the lines of corporate governance would be useful in establishing guidelines for PSE governance" (NCAER, 2004: 6). Having said that, enterprises also felt that members of thc Ad-Hoc Task Force (ATF) should be armed with technical expertise which would be essential to factor in issues confronting the industry.

With respect to output, the study makes it clear that the enterprises felt that the MoU failed in one of its most important function, which is to reduce 'administrative direction'. Enterprises further felt that the MoU was a sign of intent from the government to foster concepts like 'Strategic Business Unit' and 'MBO' within the PSEs. Another view that emerged from the enterprises is that the where the MoU succeeded, in playing an important role in improving static functions such as, profitability, investment, improved inventory management, overhead cost reduction and increased production, it failed to have a similar positive influence on dynamic and efficiency factors such as, development of new products, processes and organisational innovations.

The outcome, according to the study, reveals that the MoU system has a wide-reaching impact on the PSE and in the case of some enterprises the brand equity would be determined on the basis of the rating the enterprise receives in the MoUs. The enterprises also voiced their pleasure that the system contributed to the top and middle management becoming more analytical and articulate.

And finally, several different suggestions are documented by the study, made by the enterprises to further improve the system. One of the suggestions supported by many PSEs is the 'Business Group Review', which is the model where experts from similar functional groups review the performance of other units. Another opinion voiced is to alter the incentive system which existed at the time and the need to link the performance of the enterprises under the MoU system with a monetary incentive system which s clear and unambiguous. According to the study, most of the enterprises were against penalties in case of poor performance of enterprises under the MoU system and that the incentives must be only in the form of monetary incentives.

Another significant suggestion going forward with the MoU system, as suggested by the enterprises,was the process of finalising the MoU. Most of the employees believed that this process should be a bottoms-up approach and consultations with the internal sections of the organisation is a must before drafting MoUs.

Impact of the MoU System

One of the main focus areas of the study was to evaluate the performance of the PSEs after the implementation of the MoU system. In order to revamp the MoU system, the study first attempted to understand what impact the MoU system had on the performance of the enterprises. Total Factor Productivity (TFP) approach is used to gauge the impact of the MoU instrument not just on the financial front but also on the productivity of the PSEs. A select number of PSEs (26 in total) were chosen to apply the TFP model. Thereafter, Average Annual Growth Rate (AAGR) in TFP for the pre- and post-MoU period for the enterprises was computed to check whether the MoU had an impact on the AAGR of TFP after the implementation of the system.

A comparative analysis of financial performance for the pre-and post MoU period was also done to supplement the TFP analysis.

The study examines the trends in Total Factor Productivity Growth (TFPG) syndicate-wise to look at the impact of the MoU system. The different syndicates and the change in TFPG as analysed by the study are as follows (NCAER, 2004: 23):

i) Mining and Metals Syndicate: There was no significant difference in the pre- and post AAGR of productivity in the PSEs in this syndicate.

ii) Electronics and Communications Syndicate: The PSEs in this syndicate too,the study observed,did not see any significant change in AAGR in the pre- and post MoU periods.

iii) Heavy Industry Syndicate: Here again no significant difference in the AAGR of productivity was observed in the two periods before and after MoU implementation.

iv) Process Industry Syndicate: No significant difference in the AAGR of productivity for the pre-and post MoU period.

v) Trading and Services Syndicate: No significant difference in the AAGR of productivity for the pre-and post MoU period.

vi) Financial Services: No significant difference in the AAGR of productivity for the pre- and post-MoU period.

vii) Consultancy Services Syndicate: No significant difference in the AAGR of productivity for the pre- and post MoU period.

The study also does a TFPG and AAGR analysis on the PSEs based on the nature of their business like manufacturing and services and still found no significant change in the AAGR of productivity for the pre-and post MoU periods. Concluding that there was not enough justification from the empirical evidence to conclusively say that the introduction of the MoU system improved the productivity of the enterprises, the study says that for each of the syndicates,the performance of the post MoU period actually deteriorated. The study enumerates several possible causes for this peculiar results, such as, the indicators in the MoU are predominantly financial indicators and don't reflect the improvement in the productivity. Another cause is the timing of the introduction of the MoU system which coincided with the period of liberalisation and reforms in the markets which increased the competition for the enterprises as the sectors were opened up for private players as well, which could be the reason for the low or negative performance.

The financial performance comparison revealed a differing result with the productivity analysis. The study concluded the analysis of the financial parameters revealed that the MoU had a favourable impact on the performance of the PSEs with regards to the financial parameters although the productivity of the enterprises did not improve much.

Qualitative Indicators versus Quantitative indicators

A paradox encountered in their impact study of the PSEs in the pre- and post MoU periods. The PSEs were found to be performing well in improving their financial parameters post the implementation of the MoU system but did not show any significant improvement in their productivity. It was against this back ground that the study sought to evolve static (quantitative) parameters and dynamic (qualitative) parameters, re-design the weightages that are attributed to the different sets of parameters and also re-design the proportional weight that each group of parameters are assigned in a bid to redesign the MoU to more adequately measure both the financial and productivity indicators.

Accordingly, overall weights assigned to static and dynamic indicators were rearranged for PSEs operating in all sectors except financial,trading,consulting and social sectors in the following manner (NCAER, 2004: 42):

i) Static Financial Parameters: Static parameters would carry 50 per cent weight in the MoU. The indicators in this group included:

   a) Financial Performance Indicators: Profit Related
      1) Gross Margin/Gross Block.
      2) Net Profit/Net Worth.
      3) Gross profit/Capital Employed.
   b) Financial Indicators: Size Related
      1) Gross margin.
      2) Gross sales.
   c) Financial Return Indicators:
      1) PBDT/ Total Employment.
      2) Added Value.

ii) Dynamic Factors: These set of indicators combined were to carry 30 per cent of the weightage. The indicators in this category included:

a) Quality (ISO certification, internalisation of quality within SBU/products).
b) Customer satisfaction (customer orientation).
c) HRD (employee satisfaction & motivation).
d) R&D/For sustained and continuous innovation.
e) Project implementation (modernisation and expansion).
f) Capital expenditure/Greenfield investments/joint ventures.
g) Extent of globalisation.

iii) Sector Specific Variable: Assigned 10 per cent of the weightage. To be decide by Task force on consultation with PSEs

iv) Enterprise Specific Variable: Assigned 10 per cent of the weightage. To be decide by Task Force on consultation with PSEs

Similarly, indicators and weightages for indicators were assigned separately for the financial, trading and social sectors.

The study suggests redistribution in the priorities of the PSEs. Qualitative indicators are given almost equal weightages as the quantitative indicators laying more emphasis on the productivity or dynamic performance of a PSE along with the financial or static performance. This is one of the major recommendations and many of the changes suggested in the study in this regards can be found in the MoU documents even today.

Working Group on Review of MoU Guidelines in CPSE

This committee headed by Shri Ashok Chandra, in 2008 (GoI and DPE, 2008), submitted the report which was of vital importance in the context of the MoU in India. The report emphasised the importance of the public sector which grew from just 5 enterprises with a combined investment of ₹29 crore at the time of the First Five Year Plan to 2006-07, when the same public sector stood at 217 operating CPSEs accounting for a total investment of ₹4,21,089 crore. The main scope of the working group was the improving of the new methodology for performance evaluation adopted by the Department of Public Enterprises (DPE) in 2004-05.

The working group deals with some very pertinent questions relating to the MoU. Some of important aspects looked at by the committee are:

i) Determination of basic targets and difference between different grades on the 5 point scale.
ii) Review the balance score card approach of giving equal weights to financial and non-financial parameters.
iii) Distinguishing the performance of large and small firms through size related criteria/parameters.
iv) Review of the criteria for performance evaluation.
v) Review of the syndicates of task force under the MoU system.
vi) Appropriate mechanism for reflecting targets and performance of subsidiaries and joint ventures in the targets and performance of the holding companies.

The group was trying to refine and fine tune the functioning of the MoU system in India through improving the methodology of performance evaluation. And the main areas where it felt there was need for improvement was in the target setting process and determination of weights of the different types of parameters/criteria. The previous committee report we looked at touched upon the criteria selection, this report too looks at the criteria for performance evaluation.

Basic Targets

The committee observes that at the time, estimated achievements of the MoU signing year were being used to set targets for performance evaluation in the MoU for that year. Such estimates would have to come from the CPSEs themselves and hence, there was a general apprehension that the projections made by the CPSEs would be soft targets or distorted targets to suit their convenience and so the system prevalent was not seen as being a very reliable one. The recommendation was made to change the targets setting methods to take into account the performance of the enterprises for the preceding five years of the MoU year. As many felt that estimates should not be the basis for setting future targets.

The committee recommended that the appropriate method to calculate the basic target (B.T.) would be to take into account the actual performance of the enterprise for the previous five years. Calculate the standard deviation (S.D.) for the five years. And also the best performance figure in the last five years should be identified. The B.T. would be the sum of the best performance year plus twice the S.D. However, if in case the estimated performance for the current year or the projected figure for the next year are higher than the figure arrived at by using the performance of the last five years, then, the those figures would be used as basic targets.

Once the B.T. is set, the next question would be–where to place it. The committee suggests the placement of the B.T. must differ for enterprises which are not functioning at 100 per cent capacity and enterprises which are functioning at 100 per cent capacity utilisation. For the former, the B.T. would be placed in the 'Good' column and for the latter, the B.T. would be placed in the 'Very Good' column. What this effectively does is that the enterprises which are not performing at 100 per cent capacity utilisation are encouraged to perform well beyond their best performance figures for the last five years to be classified as 'Very Good'. And for the enterprises that do function at 100 per cent capacity, they have to perform slightly better than the performance levels of the previous years.

The next step would be to determine the targets in the other columns in the 5 grade system. The columns to the left of the B.T. the figure of S.D. or 5 per cent of B.T, whichever is higher, is added. While for columns to the right of the B.T. the figure of S.D. or 5 per cent,whichever is lower, is deducted. Also to be added to the B.T. figure would be new capacities that have just come up or are likely to come up in the MoU year.

Balance Score Card

While the committee felt that there is merit in the balance score card method of 50-50 ratio of financial to non-financial parameters, it cannot be applied uniformly to all CPSEs. For example, CPSEs which would have to function in different types of markets and also it would be difficult to use the balance score card approach for CPSEs which may not entirely be commercial in nature. It was suggested that the weight given for financial parameters should be kept below 50 per cent in the following types of CPSEs:

i) Where freedom of action of CPSE is circumscribed by a conscious decision or directive of the government.
ii) CPSEs are expected to break new ground or concentrate its efforts in areas which may not yield the best possible results.
iii) CPSEs working with social objectives and catering to the requirement s of the disadvantaged classes.

The committee recommends that for enterprises operating in an administrated pricing regime but is more or less working in a sector which is by and large reserved for the public sector,the weightage of the financial parameters can be reduced to 40 per cent in relation to the non-financial parameters. The committee further recommends a reduction of financial weights to 30 per cent in CPSEs which operate in a sector which has private players also participating and yet has to function in an administered pricing regime. It was left to the discretion of the Syndicate Group to adjudicate the final weights of the financial parameters in the abovementioned CPSEs. In the case of CPSEs operating in the social and financial sectors also the financial parameters were to be reduced to 30 per cent of the total weight. And finally, the committee accounts for other CPSEs like section 25 companies for which the weightages attached for financial parameters to be 30 per cent and no weightage for financial parameters for CPSEs under construction.

Size Related Criteria

With respect to the size related criteria, the committee says just simple size of the enterprise cannot be criteria for allocating weights in MoUs. But the geographical spread, monopoly market (competition), activities undertaken by the CPSEs, targets and objectives would be better indicators than simply using size as a parameter. A suggestion is made for a much more in-depth and detailed study to define parameters and allocate weights to it, deeming it unnecessary to introduce size related parameters.

Offsets and Performance Evaluation

Offsets are to be taken into account selectively and at the evaluation stage. This is a suggestion which was to improve the evaluation process of the enterprises. The committee feels that the syndicate groups must be allowed to take into account various major developments to make the evaluation process more rational, like force majeure,government directives and scanty rainfall etc., which are factors that could not have been foreseen or anticipated. The following facts have to be established for offsets to be accepted (GoI and DPE, 2008: 32):

i) The development is of a major nature;
ii) That it has impacted the MoUs targets in a way that the CPSE could not have made up the shortfall in any way;
iii) The effects are identifiable and measurable.

The committee cautions the syndicate groups to give allowance only in the rarest of rare cases so as to avoid using these offsets to explain away non-performance.

Composition of Syndicates

With respect to the composition of the syndicate, the committee, leaving the decision in this regard with the DPE, suggests some general pointers such as, having a small and cohesive group of seven or eight members in each syndicate and also to have a diversified membership in the syndicates consisting of management experts, economists, chartered accountants, ex-bureaucrats and ex-CMDs. This would enable the syndicate group to have a better standing and working knowledge during negotiations with the enterprises.

Task Force Members and MoU Finalisation

The committee notes, in its report, that it was a common occurrence that members did not take part in the negotiation meetings. It is recommended that any member of the task force who misses more than two MoU negotiation meetings must not be retained in the next year of the respective MoU cycle year.

A second recommendation is made with regard to the finalisation of the MoU, where it is suggested that the MoU finalisation must be done in two meeting. The first meeting would be for the general discussions on issue, priorities and targets, etc. The second meetings would involve all the parties coming together to share their feedback and finalise the final draft of the MoU.

Performance Evaluation of Subsidiary Companies

The committee feels it is important for the performance of the subsidiary company's performance to also be evaluated and reflected in the MoU of the holding company when the entire performance of the of the holding company depends on the performance of its subsidiaries. It is deemed unnecessary and even impractical to incorporate the performance of the subsidiaries or joint ventures in normal circumstances.

It is suggested that in the cases where the performance of the subsidiaries, joint ventures or share holding subsidiaries has no major impact on the performance of the holding company, around 5 per cent of the weightage in the basic MoU must be allocated to the following (GoI and DPE, 2008):

i) 1 per cent: Has the CPSE executed MoUs with all its subsidiaries (it gets zero if the answer is no).
ii) 1 per cent: Have the MoUs with the subsidiaries been evaluated (zero if the answer is no).
iii) 1 per cent: If 60 per cent or more of the subsidiaries get an excellent evaluation report (zero if it is less than 60 per cent).
iv) 1 per cent: If 75 per cent or more of the subsidiaries get a very good or better evaluation report (zero if the figure is less than 75 per cent).
v) 1 per cent: If 100 per cent subsidiaries get a good or better evaluation report (zero if the figure is less than 100 per cent)

The committee also recommends that the MoUs between holding companies and subsidiary companies should be along the same lines as the MoU between the government and the CPSEs.

Report of Panel of Experts on Reforms in Central Public Sector Enterprises (CPSEs), 2011

The committee traces the evolution of the MoU system and also discusses the problems with the system in 2011 and the recommendations which the committee makes are:

i) While recommending the continuation of the MoU system, the committee felt that some basic changes had to be made to the system to make them more effective as the system that was operating till then was formulated when the PEs were operating in a regulated environment.

ii) The committee felt that the MoU system would have to go beyond just a performance evaluation tool and would have to transcend into an instrument which would give the enterprises a direction to their business and business processes. The MoU would have to account for diversification, acquisition, formation of JVs, new/strategic businesses, usage of ICT, R&D initiatives, HRD and organisational changes, etc., as the enterprises approach these processes to stay competitive in the market.

iii) MoUs to be delinked from Performance Related Pay (PRP).

iv) Benchmarking with industrial parameters including the private sector for physical parameters, if any, in the MoU.

Report of the Committee on the MoU System

The Committee headed by Shri P.G. Mankad[5] had several recommendations with regards to:

i) Formats: Where it was suggested that the system of multiple formats be replaced with uniform formats with built in flexibility taking into account enterprise/sector specific factors.

ii) Target setting: Basic Targets and differences in rating should be at the discretion of the Task Force. DPE should also bring out glossary and definitions of financial and accounting terms

5. *Report of the Committee on the MoU System*. GoI & Ministry of Heavy Industries & Public Enterprises & DPE, 2012.

used in MoU documents. As for the non-financial targets, the parameters should be divided under heads such as: Corporate Social Responsibility & Sustainable Development, R&D, technology, quality and innovation, etc. A case is also made by the committee to introduced negative marking for non-compliance with DPE guidelines for CPSEs on an experimental basis.

iii) MoU guidelines: The committee was satisfied with the guidelines being issued by the DPE and felt that it was comprehensive. But points out that the guidelines would have to be revised in light of the changes proposed by the committee.

iv) MoU and RFD system: This is an important recommendation made by the committee as far as the integration of the two systems. The committee felt that the issue of harmonising, synchronisation and synergy of the MoU and RFD system which the DPE faces can only be addressed at the government level and the DPE is asked to take it up with the High Powered Committee which is a group of secretaries headed by the Cabinet Secretariat.

Current Scenario of the MoU System

The number of enterprises signing MoUs, have increased exponentially since it was first introduced in 1987-88. The first year of the MoU system, saw four enterprises signing the instrument on an experimental basis, based on the French system of performance contracting. Since then, the number of enterprises signing MoUs has gone up to 195 in 2012-13. Table 2.1 shows the increase in MoU signing enterprises since its beginning.

Institutional Mechanisms

The institutional mechanism for implementation of the MoU system has been refined and fine tuned over the years, and has changed over the years. The extant institutional mechanism for the MoU system is:

i) High Powered Committee (HPC): The HPC is the apex committee in the MoU system and is a Committee of Secretaries (CoS). The HPC is charged with assessing the performance of the MoU signing CPSEs against the targets set in the MoU. Along with this, the HPC is also charged with assessing how far the administrative ministries/departments have succeeded in keeping their end of the commitments as promised in the MoU. The body is headed by the Cabinet Secretary, GoI. The Member-Secretary of the committee is the Secretary, DPE.

Table 2.1

MoU Signing Enterprises (Year-wise Data)

Year	*MoU Signing Enterprises*
1987-88	4
1991-92	72
2001-02	104
2002-03	100
2003-04	96
2004-05	99
2005-06	102
2006-07	113
2007-08	144
2008-09	147
2009-10	197
2010-11	202
2011-12	197
2012-13	195

Source: Department of Public Enterprises, *Annual Survey 2012-13.*

ii) Task Force: The task force is charged with target setting and assigning weightages to parameters, along with evaluation of performance of the CPSEs. The members of the Task Force include ex-Civil servants, ex-Chief Executives of CPSEs, Professisonals and academicians from relevant disciplines. The task force has sub-groups called syndicates, each of which is charged with managing CPSEs in a specific sector.

In the extant system, CPSEs were categorised into 12 syndicates, each normally comprising 5-6 members, headed by a convenor, SD expert, Finance/CA expert, CSR expert, R&D expert and human resource management expert. In 2012-13, there were 68 Task Force members and 1 chairman.

Target Setting and Performance Evaluation

The process of target setting and evaluation begins with the DPE, as follows:

i) Release of the MoU guidelines in the month of October/ November.

ii) Preparation of draft MoUs on the basis of the guidelines, which are then submitted to the administrative ministries.

iii) Examination of draft MoUs by the MoU division of the DPE and the subsequent circulation of the critiques to be handed over to the members of the task force.

iv) Scheduling of MoU negotiation meetings that begin from January/February.

v) Negotiation meetings to finalise the MoUs with the Task Force (Janurary-March) each year.

vi) Preparation and circulation of minutes.

vii) Draft of MoU by CPSEs on the basis of minutes.

viii) Evaluation of MoU by the task force members as submitted by CPSEs and vetted by DPE.

ix) All MoUs have to be signed before 31st March of every year.[6]

MoU Guidelines and Evaluation

Every year the MoU division issues the MoU guidelines, taking into account the dynamic and complex environment in which the public enterprises operate in. Based on the guidelines every year, the CPSEs prepare draft MoUs and from there the MoU is negotiated and

6 *Public Enterprises Survey 2011-12 (http://dpe.nic.in/sites/upload_files/dpe/files/survey1112/survey01/vol1ch8.pdf)*

finally the MoU is signed. The MoU guidelines form the first step of the MoU cycle. They cover every aspect of the MoU such as:

i) Applicability.
ii) Exemptions from MoU.
iii) Guiding principles for setting targets.
iv) Financial targets (static parameters).
v) Financial targets.
vi) Non-financial targets.
vii) Group targets.
viii) Revision of targets.
ix) Task Force/Expert group.
x) Meeting of Standing Committee.
xi) Participation by administrative ministry/CPSEs.
xii) Pre-negotiation meeting of Task Force.
xiii) Timelines.

We look at the MoU guidelines for 2015-16[7] to analyse the target setting and determination of targets in the MoU guidelines.

The guidelines for the year 2015-16 make it clear upfront, that the evaluation process is based on the 'Balance Score Card' approach. It is a combination of financial and non-financial targets, having equal weightage in the overall scores. In the case of sick and loss making enterprises, the guidelines try to focus more on the non-financial indicators rather than the financial indicators, and they slightly alter the ratio of the financial to non-financial weights to 40-60 per cent respectively.

The five point scale to grade the enterprises are the same—enterprises are rated 'excellent' to 'poor', based on the score they receive in the MoU score. The basic targets and the difference between the different ratings are subject to negotiation and fixing of targets in consultation with the Task Force, CPSEs and the administrative ministries.

---

7. *MoU Guidelines 2015-16 (http://www.dpeMoU.nic.in/MoUFiles/MoU_GL_2015-16.pdf)*

Financial Targets

Financial targets are specified and defined in the guidelines by the DPE and all CPSEs are expected to adhere to these while choosing the financial targets, without any deviation. A self certification is to be filled out by the CPSEs to this effect, and even in the instance that the CPSEs are found not to have adhered with the targets,the evaluation of the financial parameters will still be calculated in accordance with the definitions provided by the DPE.

As for the targets themselves, the guidelines are clear that the financial targets should be: (i) realistic, (ii) growth oriented, and (iii) aspirational.

The targets must be, at the same time, consistent with the budget for the respective year, and in conformity with those made by the Planning Commission, Ministry of Finance, administrative ministry/ department and other statutory and regulatory bodies. In instances where the CPSEs are found to be under-pitching, the Task Force or the DPE will have the liberty to call upon the CMD of the CPSEs to give explanations for such under-pitching, or gross over achievement.

The basic targets are to be arrived at based on a combination of the performance of the enterprise over five preceding years, and other factors such as: (i) capacity and its expansion; (ii) business environment; (iii) projects under implementation; (iv) government policies; (v) external factors; and (vi) company's growth forecast.[8]

Another important factor to be considered for the basic financial targets, is the national/international benchmarking. Benchmarking is not applicable for all the enterprises, and so it is to be considered for the enterprises for which it is applicable.

In the extant MoU system, the basic targets are generally expected to be an ambitious growth over the performance of the enterprise in the preceding year, however, if the performance of the enterprise is found to be bad in the previous year, then a more realistic target, based on the average performance of the previous three years, is to be taken into account.

8. *MoU Guidelines 2015-16 (http://www.dpeMoU.nic.in/MoUFiles/MoU_GL_2015-16.pdf)*

Non-Financial/Dynamic Targets

The non-financial targets are a little more difficult to determine and the guidelines specify that non-financial targets must be SMART (specific, measurable, attainable, result-oriented, tangible). Non-financial targets in the MoU should be in the following categories:

i) Sector specific and enterprise specific targets.
ii) Initiatives for growth.
iii) Capacity addition.
iv) Project management and implementation.
v) CAPEX: capital expenditure.
vi) Corporate social responsibility (CSR) and sustainability.
vii) Research and development.
viii) Human resource management.
ix) Risk management.

Corporate governance is a very important aspect in the existing system of MoU, where there are negative marks and penalties in scores for any enterprise found to be in non-compliance of the corporate governance norms, which were specified by the DPE, and for listed companies, also specified the SEBI guidelines. Similar penalties and negative markings are also applicable to the non-compliance of the CSR guidelines, DPE guidelines and other forms of non-compliance.

Grading

The MoU system when first introduced, was based on the French Contracting System and it was later changed to the Signaling System after a year and after 2004-05, it was further refined to the BSC approach.

Performance of the enterprises in the MoU system is scored on a 5 point index, which is calculated as the aggregate of all the actual achievements as against the targets set in the 5 point scale. The grading is done based in the MoU Composite Score as detailed below:

MoU Composite Score	*Rating*
87.5 to 100	Excellent
Less than 87.5 – 67.5	Very Good
Less than 67.5 – 37.5	Good
Less than 37.5 – 12.5	Fair
Less than 12.5	Poor

Performance Related Pay (PRP)

The incentives system is an integral part of the present system of MoU. The incentives system has two components: monetary and non-monetary incentives. These incentives combine to form part of the core aims and objectives of the system for CPSEs, like:

i) Increasing the autonomy of management of the company.
ii) Removing fuzziness in goals and objectives of the enterprises.
iii) To evaluate the performance of the managers in the public enterprises.
iv) To provide incentives for better performance in the future.

The present system of incentives or PRP was conceptualised in the Second Pay Revision Committee report. According to the recommendations of the Committee, the variable PRP would be available to profit making CPSEs, in accordance with their MoU rating. A 100 per cent eligibility for CPSEs achieving 'excellent' rating, 80 per cent eligibility for rating of 'very good', 60 per cent for 'good' and 40 per cent for 'fair' rating of basic pay. The CPSEs with 'poor' rating for the MoU year will not be eligible for PRP for that year.[9]

One of the important recommendations made by the committee is that it should be mandatory for all CPSEs to sign MoUs with their administrative ministries and secondly, it is also recommended that CPSEs not signing MoUs should not be eligible for PRP.

Prior to the introduction of the PRP system, CPSE employees had been paid the entire compensation, which was guaranteed irrespective of the enterprise performance or individual performance. The earlier

9. *Public Enterprises Survey 2011-12 (http://dpe.nic.in/sites/upload_files/dpe/files/survey1112/survey01/vol1ch8.pdf)*

system was at odds with compensation in the private sector. In the private sector, a large portion of the compensation paid to individual employees has a variable component, which is reflective of their contribution to the company's performance. The Second Pay Revision committee recommends that a similar system be introduced in the public sector enterprises as well. The variable component itself would vary at the different levels of management in the enterprises, where the low level executives have a relatively low variable component which would increase as the individual is higher up the hierarchy.[10]

Table 2.2

PRP as Percentage of Basic Pay

Grade	*A+, A, B Categories*	*C & D Categories*
E0 to E1	40	40
E2 to E3	40	40
E4 to E5	50	50
E6 to E7	60	60
E8 to E9	70	70
E10	100	—
Director	150	100
CMD	200	150

Source: Second Pay Revision Committee vide DPE OM No. 2(70)/08-DPE (WC)-GL-XV/08 dtd. 26.11.2008 (*http://dpe.nic.in/sites/upload_files/dpe/files/Chapter_6_Recommendations_Final.pdf*)

The committee also makes recommendations regarding the PRP to individuals and groups, based on their performance and need to develop a comprehensive Performance Management System (PMS). Since PRP to individuals and groups will be based on performance against Key Result Areas, the committee recommends that all CPSEs should develop a robust and transparent PMS. CPSEs should adopt 'Bell curve approach' in grading the officers, so that not more than 10 to 15 per cent executives are outstanding/excellent. Similarly 10 per cent of executives should be graded as below par.[11]

---

10. Second Pay Revision Committee vide DPE OM No. 2(70)/08-DPE (WC)-GL-XV/08 dtd. 26.11.2008 (*http://dpe.nic.in/sites/upload_files/dpe/files/Chapter_4_Paradigm%20Shift_Final.pdf*)

11. Ibid. (*http://dpe.nic.in/sites/upload_files/dpe/files/Chapter_6_Recommendations_Final.pdf*)

According to the committee, the PRP itself would be drawn from the Profit Before Tax (PBT) and the same would be linked to the individual, group, business unit and company performance. The determination of the amount of the variable payments would be linked to the MoU system in CPSEs, and so it is recommended that the signing of MoU should be made mandatory for all CPSEs. The variable payments for companies as well as executives would be determined conditional on achieving pre-determined physical, as well as, financial targets. The companies would have to internalise the MoU process upto the lowest operative level.[12]

The PRP would come out of the profits of the company, based on physical and financial performance in accordance with the methodology suggested by the committee, where 60 per cent of the performance pay would be given with a ceiling of 3 per cent PBT, and 40 per cent of PRP would come out of 10 per cent of incremental profit. And the total PRP would be limited to 5 per cent of the year's PBT. The committee recommends that for individual levels of PRP, the methodology can be finalised by the CPSE concerned. It is suggested that the enterprises put in place, a rational and transparent Performance Management System, internally, which would be decided by the CPSE. Balanced score cards would also have to be introduced to determine the eligibility of PRP for each executive.[13]

Effective 9 February 2009, a circular was issued by the DPE, informing CPSEs to follow the recommendation and methodology as suggested by the Second Pay Revision Committee report, regarding the PRP.[14]

12. Ibid. (*http://dpe.nic.in/sites/upload_files/dpe/files/Chapter_4_Paradigm%20Shift_)*

13. Ibid. *(http://dpe.nic.in/sites/upload_files/dpe/files/Chapter_6_Recommendations_Final.pdf)*

14. Revision of Pay Scales of Executives of Central Public Enterprises (CPSEs) W.E.F 01.01.2007–Performance Management System (PMS)-Linkage of Performance Related Pay (PRP) with MoU Rating of CPSEs and Performance of Individual Executives vide OM No. 2(70)/08-DPE (WC)-GL IV/09.

References

GoI and DPE (2008). *The Working Group on Review of MoU Guidelines in CPSEs.*

GoI, Ministry of Heavy Industries & Public Enterprises and DPE (2012). *Report of the Committee on the MoU System.*

NCAER (2004). *Study on the Revamping of the MoU System.* p.2.

3

Setting Performance Targets and MoU System

Introduction

Performance contracts (PCs) have been adopted by governments globally as tools to enhance performance of their SOEs (state-owned enterprises). A study conducted by the World Bank shows that more than 32 developing countries adopted the system of PCs and they have been termed differently by different countries like contract- plan in France, MoU (memorandum of understanding) in India, signaling system in Pakistan and so on (Shirley, 1995). All these contracts are negotiated and written agreements between governments and their enterprises with mutually agreed targets which the enterprises achieve within a given time frame. The system also defines the mechanisms for evaluating the performance within the specified period within a pre-determined institutional framework.

PCs have been broadly classified under two systems—the French based systems and the signaling system. The French system was followed by France, Africa (Senegal, Benin and Morocco), and Latin America. Under this system, weights were not allocated to the targets which added a high degree of subjectivity to the evaluation process. In the signaling system, signals were sent to the managers in order to monitor the results of the contacts. This system originated in Pakistan and Korea, and was adopted by many Asian countries (Pakistan, South Korea, and Bangladesh), Africa (Ghana, Nigeria, and Gambia) and Latin America. Initially, the MoU system adopted in India was based on the line of French system; during its evolution many features from the signaling system were adopted. Currently, the MoU signed between the PEs (public enterprises) and the ministries consists of mission of the enterprise, its objectives, performance criteria, weightages assigned to each criteria and the period of contract and the mode of evaluation. For any measurement system there are certain identified criteria which reflects the health of the system and they are termed as performance indicators. In the case of MoU system both financial indicators like profit, sales etc., are used while non-financial indicators include human resource management, project implementation, research and development etc. The Balanced Scorecard (BSC) is a strategy performance management tool—a semi-standard structured report, supported by design methods and automation tools that can be used by managers to keep track of the execution of activities by the staff within their control and to monitor the consequences arising from these actions..

The role and importance of these enterprises in a national economic growth changed considerably from being mere tools of fulfilling social objectives to being growth engines and contributing to economic prosperity of a nation. With the onset of the global financial crisis in 2008, for some countries, especially among the resource-rich emerging economies, the SOEs represented their main source of international capital as they accounted for one-fifth of international mergers and acquisitions (Mehdi, 1985). Globally, the SOEs have emerged as an important source of international investment.

There are some inherent problems that go along with these enterprises; they are usually very large in size with multiple control and accountability points which make them very difficult to govern. Therefore, the system of PCs was introduced at a time when many governments were facing troubles in managing performance of their enterprises. In this paper, we will focus on target setting process which is a key component of performance contracting system.

Target Setting Process

As a part of the process of PCs, targets are set for both financial and non-financial parameters which are based on what the enterprise can reasonably achieve, given the expected policy environment, market situation, capital expenditures, and the level of delegation of financial powers to the enterprise. For each indicator a range of values is set so that performance can be graded, e.g., excellent, good, fair, poor or bad. There are some established methods for setting enterprise targets (United Nations, 1995).

i) Inter-firm comparison: Comparison of different firms in terms of their performance and profitability. Such a type of comparison is possible only when uniform costing is applied by all the firms which forms a basis for comparison. The accumulated data regarding costs, prices, profits etc., of different concerns are put in the form of consolidated statements and are made available to all the member-units so that they can make a comparative assessment of their achievements and weaknesses with those of others. This type of comparison helps in improving efficiency wherein each member-unit comes to know about its weak points and can try to improve its efficiency in comparison with other member-firms. However, one of the key requirements of this method is the need for complete information.

ii) International comparisons of firms are not easy, because of differences in market conditions, regulatory environments of each country. It is also not possible to compare firms with other firms for monopoly enterprise, except when they are broken up regionally and the regional bodies can be compared. A combination of methods may be used for assessing PEs in each period.

   a) Trend analysis could be a basis for assessing performance improvement. If performance contracting is conceived as an instrument for progressive improvement of performance, then past performance adjusted for exogenous change is a sufficient standard. The Korean PCs make extensive use of regression analyses of past data. Seven-year time series analysis is made for most of the quantitative indicators. From these it is possible to project the expected targets for the following years, and also the standard deviation. This method is said to simplify target setting and reduce controversy. However, it rests on the assumption that the future will be a simple projection of the past.

b) Yardstick competition is applied by a target-setter knowing the unit costs in similar enterprises. In Bangladesh, for example, a detailed system of comparing cotton textile mills is used by the Bangladesh Textile Mills Corporation. The target is set by reference to the average enterprise, or the most efficient enterprise, taking the best performance on each activity. The United Kingdom Audit Commission has a tradition of "inter-firm" comparisons of local authority performance, which indicates that such comparisons may be valid and useful, despite disputes on their interpretation (Potaraju, 2000).

c) Work study and management audit is also used to set up targets, which represents reasonably efficient performance, though this method is slow and costly. The United Kingdom Monopolies and Mergers Commission (MMC) carries out in-depth review of efficiency as required by the Department of Trade and Industry. The MMC examines the trend of performance indicators, such as unit costs and quality, and management processes for want of valid international or intra-national comparisons of performance indicators, it tends to conform to widely accepted standards of management practices.

Issues and Challenges in Target Setting

Target setting process is one of the key activities of performance contracting system. A successful enterprise which is on the path of upward movement and aspires to be a leader in industry would adopt mechanisms for identifying realistic targets. Research has found out that SOEs world over have been grappling with this issue of target setting. Broadly, the issues faced by enterprises can be categorised into the following.

Determining Performance Levels

There is a constant pressure on the management of PEs to raise the bar of performance each year. There is a general feeling among the enterprise managers that if they achieve a target in a year, their performance bar is raised in the next year. Therefore, there is a need to set realistic targets which can be achieved under given circumstances which have physical limits, such as capacity utilisation, profitability etc. Due to this, there is a tendency for the enterprises to set targets in such a way that it is very much within the reach of the enterprise. While setting targets the enterprises make sure that their targets are neither too low which are easily achievable without effort nor too high which makes them unachievable.

Information Asymmetry

Ideally PCs must reduce the information advantage that enterprises have over the government and motivate enterprise officials through rewards or penalties (such as to pay bonuses or impose penalties) to achieve the targets (Shirley, 1995). In reality, the asymmetry of information between an enterprise and ministry allows the enterprise to get the targets it wants to set for itself. This asymmetry of information is taken advantage by the enterprise managers who use this to negotiate targets that were either hard for outsiders to evaluate or easy for them to achieve. In any case, performance is hard to evaluate, e.g., when there are many targets or when targets change frequently or when negotiations drag on for so long that targets set equal to ex-post performance, the targets set can be soft.

The information advantage of the enterprise coupled with governments' failure to give the bureaucrats responsible for negotiating the contracts and evaluating results the power, resources, and status they need to face enterprise managers on a level playing field leads to poor target setting. Enterprises are, therefore, able to negotiate targets that they can achieve without making additional efforts to improve productivity. The guidelines (Potaraju, 2000) to be taken in account before setting targets are as follows:

i) Efficient target setting to be carried out in a participatory process. Without this approach, targets tend to take the form of formal directives, which are often overtly accepted and covertly resisted.

ii) Targets to be clear-cut.

iii) Targets to be neither too low nor high. This would give wrong signals to the managers.

iv) Each enterprise must be looked at in its own unique environment which must be taken into account.

v) The targets must ensure that generation of surplus is significantly more than distribution by way of bonus.

vi) Targets must take into account the social tasks which are taken up by the enterprises.

Ownership Model

The ownership model in the public sector, where politicians have many points of view and bureaucrats have many different agendas creates further problems in setting performance levels. Unlike the private companies, the public sector enterprises are susceptible to be used by political bosses for their personal benefits which may stand in contradiction to their progress to reach the declared performance targets.

Strengthening Target Setting Process

The success of the MoU exercise largely depends on the basic strength of target setting process. Such strength would largely depend on the initiatives outlined as under.

Generating Continuous Research Evidence

Research evidence must be generated continuously for companies to set realistic as well as competitive targets as per their contracts. Empirical studies are carried out by countries to analyse the effect of such contracts on profitability and productivity, and examine statistically the correlation between PCs and productivity so that evidence can be generated whether PCs can actually improve efficiency. A study conducted by the World Bank (Shirley, 1995) found no pattern of improvement associated with the PCs in productivity or profitability trends. The study found no robust, positive association between PCs and productivity. An important question needs to be raised here: Is it possible that PCs failed to improve productivity? A dedicated research group or an institution must continuously be involved in data collection from SOEs, conduct research and development for the benefit of SOEs, individually and collectively, and disseminate results of study to all.

Strengthening Governance Mechanisms

Improving governance mechanisms go a long way in streamlining enterprise performance. Restructuring the board, which is the driving force behind the success of an enterprise, is very critical. Research has shown that professionalising the board improves the overall performance of enterprises especially in terms of achievement against the PCs. For example, Chile took up a successful experience in reforming its state enterprises and improving its efficiency as indicated below (Johnson and Beiman, 2007):

i) Chile increased competition by ending state monopolies and barriers to entry, reducing import tariffs to 10 per cent across the board, breaking up monopolies in sectors such as electricity, and pushing state enterprises to contract out competitive activities under strict rules of competitive bidding.
ii) It placed state enterprises under private commercial law, and members of the boards of directors became liable for their decisions.
iii) Private parties were named to boards, and boards were kept small (five people) to reduce the political value of keeping companies public.
iv) The government eliminated all subsidies, transfers, and government guarantees for debts of state enterprises, and instructed banks to lend to them under the same criteria as for private enterprises.
v) State enterprises were required to pay a 10 per cent return on assets as a dividend, and money losers were required to sell assets to pay their dividend.

Stakeholder Participation

Stakeholder participation is the key for efficient target setting. Targets should be negotiated between the government and management and should not be imposed. The benefits of participation are not confined to the government management interface. It is apparent that improvement of performance can arise only by changes in behaviour at the operating level. Therefore, there should be an internal dialogue through all levels of the enterprise extending corporate goal and incentives to all divisions and sections of the enterprise.

Period of Contract

Period of contract is equally critical for efficiency in target setting process. Planning encompasses a future period of time necessary to fulfil targets through a series of actions and commitments made and the availability of the capital.

In Gambia, for instance, PCs have been in practice for four years. They spell out the goals of the enterprise as also the autonomy of the management. The targets are separately negotiated each year and signed at the technical level. These are the basis on which annual performance is evaluated and rewarded or penalised.

In India, targets are made annually coinciding with the Annual Plans of the enterprises. While some production companies accepted the time span of one year, the companies which are in the construction and exploration business express their views differently. They prefer the contracts to be for a longer period at least for 24-36 months, which is minimum time period for completion of a project.

Strengthening Feedback Loop

Performance contracting is a cyclical process in which results are fed back to the government and public enterprise. This is done in order to make correction for short-term variances from contract and this process is called monitoring. This could be represented by the feedback loop of control.

Using Comprehensive Evaluation Tools

Economic Value Added (EVA)

EVA is a tool designed to give managers of SOEs better information to make decisions that create greatest shareholder wealth.While EVA implementation has been mainly studied in Western companies from the perspective of improving economic efficiency, we look at the great possibility of introducing EVA as a part of Performance Management System (PMS). Studies reveal that some changes in managerial behaviour have also been seen with EVA implementation (Li, 2012).

An EVA-based performance assessment policy was introduced by the State-owned Assets Supervision and Administration Commission of the State Council (SASAC), for 129 Chinese SOEs under direct administration of Central government since 2010 as a part of the mission set out for SOEs under the 11th five-year plan (2006-2010) to "grow bigger and stronger". The study shows that by the end of 2010, the net profit achieved by the 122 Central SOEs reached 848.89 billion yuan, sizeable given that total profit by all China's SOEs was 21.37 billion yuan in 1998. The Central SOEs listed in the Fortune 500 have increased from 6 in 2003 to 38 in 2011.

According to the requirement of management by objectives, SASAC adopted following performance assessment methods:

i) Annual assessment & tenure assessment.

ii) Result assessment & process evaluation.

iii) Performance outcomes & incentives: Linkage of annual assessment result with yearly merit pay, and tenure assessment result with appointment & removal as well as long-term incentives.

   a) Indicators: basic indicators and classification indicators.

   b) Objectives: maximisation of economic benefit and optimisation of asset efficiency.

   c) Principles: fewer and better indicators.

SASAC attempted to apply EVA into the annual assessment in 2007, and put it in practice in 2010.

Annual assessment = EVA (40%) + Total profit (30%) + Classification indicator A (15%) + Classification indicator B (15%)

SASAC as investor should encourage Central SOEs to emphasise on value-creating and maximising shareholder value, while EVA can play an important role in the process.

In comparision to world leading companies,Chinese Central SOEs are less competitive in value-creating and some of them are impulsive in scale expansion.

EVA is the balance found by deducting the cost of capital from the net operating profit after tax (NOPAT), which reflects value created for shareholders in a certain period. Different from traditional financial indicator, EVA is the economic surplus calculated from shareholders'(investors') perspective, following shareholders' way to evaluate enterprise value. EVA can be the value-creating indicator because: i) it could reflect the cost of debt capital and ii) it is calculated after deducting cost of equity capital from NOPAT.

Impact

Positive changes have been reported in Central SOEs after SASAC started applying EVA to performance assessment.

i) Build up of value management system.

ii) Prudent investment decision-making.

iii) Attaching importance to capital management.

iv) Attaching importance to research and development investment.

In 2003, NP (net profit) of 183 central SOEs was RMB140.2 bn (USD 23bn), with the rate of capital cost being 5 per cent, total EVA was only RMB 6.7bn (USD 1.1bn). In 2014, the EVA of all Central SOEs was RMB 350bn (USD58bn).

However, there is a strong criticisms regarding adoption of this system. Firstly, the critics argued that the SOEs outperformed at the expense of the private sector. Though the state enterprises advanced, the private sector rolled back. Some researchers and analysts even warn that the 1980s and 1990s reforms that unleashed China's private sector and dismantled the state-owned sector are being partly undone (Wines, 2010). Secondly, although it is hard to argue with success, the means by which China's SOEs have achieved success have been criticised. It is argued that overall SOEs produce a relatively small share of gross output and value added, but consume a large proportion of capital, raw materials and intermediate inputs relative to the private sector. The advantages that SOEs obtained from preferential access to bank finance and business opportunities, and even protection against competition, have created a profound inequality with private competitors (World Bank, 2012).

Balanced Score Card Approach

The use of BSC methodology for SOEs, is said to improve enterprise profitability. It provides required guidance to enterprise managers using modern management concepts, methods, and tools; stimulate identification, analysis, and resolution of problems interfering with improvement of enterprise performance; and most importantly builds consensus and improves communication among management, employees, and stakeholders. BSC tool is being used not only in developed economies but in transitional economies as well. Having been successfully used to drive alignment and strategic results in the private sector,g overnments are increasingly using BSC in government organisations and SOEs as part of an integrated strategy management process. Various types of SOEs use BSC tools to describe, measure, align, and manage their strategies.

Jinshan Telecom is a branch unit of China Telecom (an SOE) which uses BSC as a tool for performance enhancement (Kaplan, 2001). Jinshan Telecom has 4 sections, 17 substations, and more than 20 retail service offices. In 2001, Jinshan's performance measurement and appraisal system did not reflect company's strategic priorities. Its Key Performance Indicators (KPIs—another term used to describe the "measures") were not linked to the company's strategy. Each employee at Jinshan had 30–50 KPIs for which the employee was responsible. The numerous KPIs deterred employees from focusing on what was most strategically important. Moreover, it was difficult for the company to analyse, consolidate, or discuss the KPIs in management's efforts to execute their strategy more effectively. Further investigations found that Jinshan Telecom's cross departmental teamwork and cooperation was weak. The existing performance appraisal system lacked focus and did not align the organisation horizontally across sections. The company adopted BSC methodology and it was cascaded down to all departments and individuals. As a result, company employees had clearer objectives, measures, and performance "targets". Also, a variable pay incentive system was established while deploying the BSC methodology. This led to an increase in employee motivation for improving business results. The company achieved significant improvements in vertical and horizontal alignment, as well as significant improvements in cross-departmental teamwork and cooperation as a result of its BSC implementation.

Measurable improvements in quantitative performance, as reported by Mr Xia Pei Yun, General Manager of Jinshan Telecom, included:[1]

i) Jinshan Telecom's 2003 growth rate was more than three times the Group Company's growth rate. It grew by 14 per cent, compared to the Group Company's 4 per cent growth rate (Jinshan was the first branch unit in the group company to deploy BSC).

ii) Jinshan's superior growth rate was enabled by reaching or exceeding strategic performance targets in customer, process, and learning areas.

iii) Jinshan's results on five performance measures met or exceeded targets: key account satisfaction, commercial account satisfaction, repair cycle time, connection to internet success, and implementation of planned trainings.

Total Factor Productivity (TFP)

TFP is a composite measure of technological change and changes in the efficiency with which known technology is applied to production. The translog index of technology changes is based on a translog production function, characterisation by constant returns to scale. In this method, from with the use of two inputs: Labour (L) and Capital (K) only, TFPG can be estimated adequately. The studies show that growth in financial profitability is not necessarily always accompanied by an increase in TFP. Of the two, TFP is considered to be a superior method of evaluating performance. However, it is yet to

1. Reported in a presentation entitled, "Using the BSC to Implement Performance Management", at the First BSC Forum in China, Shanghai Jin Mao Conference Center, 19 December 2003

gain acceptability in the SOEs as it is does not support the managers' stake to high performance claim, benefit from financial incentives and projecting brighter image. The complexity of the method and lack of capacity on the part of the regulators and managers to implement it has hindered the popularity of TFP (Mishra *et al.*, 2001).

Conclusion

With the new government taking over in India in 2014, the focus has shifted on making the PEs more efficient and competitive so that they can face the stiff market competition. The MoU system is being made more transparent by using information technology and a new online MoU system is being designed and launched from the current year from October 2015-16. This system will bring in greater scope for using the enterprise data for effective planning and decision-making by the government.

References

Johnson, Christian C. and Irv Beiman (ed.) (2007). *Driving Performance and Corporate Governance.* ADB.

Kaplan, Robert (2001). *Integrating shareholder Value and Activity-based Costing with the Balanced Scorecard.* Balanced Scorecard Report.15 January.

Li, Pingli (2012). *EVA Adoption in SOEs: A Case of Revolutionary Change.* Middlesex University Business School, UK Guliang Tang, Narisa Tiangjing Dai, University of International Business and Economics, PRC, CGMA & CIMA.

Mehdi, Isteqbal (1985). "Setting Targets for Improving Cost Efficiencies in PE's", Paper Presented at a *Conference on Cost Effective Management of PE's.* Karachi. 14 July.

Mishra R.K., Nandgopal, P. Geeta and Navin Bulusu (2001). *Role of Memorandum of Understanding in Public Enterprise Reforms.* New Delhi: Vikas Publications.

Potaraju, Geeta (2000). *Memorandum of Understanding and Public Enterprises in India.* PhD Thesis submitted to Department of Business Management and Commerce, Osmania University, Hyderabad.

Shirley, Mary (1995). "Why Performance Contracts for State Owned Enterprises Haven't Worked", *World Bank Publication Note* No.150. Public Policy for the Private Sector.

United Nations (1995). *Performance Contracting for Public Enterprises.* New York: Development Support and Management Services.

4

Implementation Arrangements for MoU System in India

As a prelude to understanding the problems of PE (public enterprise), it is essential to appreciate its environment, which has far-reaching effects on the working of PE. The environment of PE is a complex phenomenon and needs to be conceptualised (Narain, 1980). It is more unpredictable and less stable as compared to a private enterprise. The reasons for this are many; the most essential one being the changing socio-political conditions which have a direct effect on the performance of the PEs. As brought out by Lord Beeching,[1] a former Chairman of the British Railways, in the following passage:

> In the case of private industry there is a single, clear and unchanging primary objective, and the management is free to optimize its behavior in pursuit of that objective within a general framework of conditions imposed by law, practice and opinion.... In the case of a nationalized industry on the other hand objectives are numerous, more ambiguous and less distinguishable....

The MoU system introduced in PSEs (public sector enterprises) can be seen in the context of the environment in which it is functioning. The PEs in India experience the maximum pull and push from all the agencies, which directly or indirectly control the working of these enterprises. The PEs being 'public', they are accountable to a number of agencies, which directly or indirectly influence the working of an enterprise (see Figure 4.1).

---

1. Lord Beeching's report "The Reshaping of British Railways", commonly referred to as "The Beeching Report", which led to far-reaching changes in the railway network, popularly known as the Beeching Axe, 1960.

The administrative ministry which is the all-in-all for a PE controls the overall working of the enterprise through a number of ways. The Planning Commission decides upon the projects to be sanctioned to the PEs and thus exercises its control. The finance ministry controls the working of a PE through its budget. The CAG and Central Vigilance Commission (CVC) also exercise their control over the PEs through their checks on expenditure.

The President, the Cabinet, and the Minister-in-charge also exercise their control over the working of the PEs. The aid-giving agencies like the World Bank and other financing agencies equally control the working of an enterprise. With all these controls, the PEs hardly finds space to work independently. The main reasons for introducing the system of MoU by the Government, following the Arjun Sengupta Committee Report in 1985, was to reduce these kind of pulls on the PEs and give them the necessary space to perform.

Figure 4.1

Various Agencies Exercising Control Over the Working of Public Enterprises in India

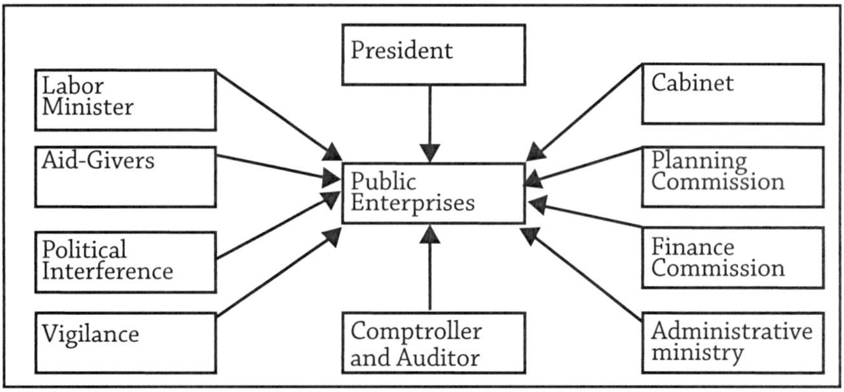

Rationale for MoU

The MoU in India is a document signed annually between the PE management and the concerned administrative ministry. The highlighting features of a PC (performance contract) in India are that it contains well defined mission, objectives and goals of the enterprise, performance criteria, weightages, target value, rating and evaluation. The contracts are made keeping in mind the mission of an enterprise on the long-term basis and the objective of the enterprise on a short-term basis. The performance criteria are decided in accordance with the objectives of an enterprise. The criteria are given weightages to indicate the relative priority of each indicator. The weights may be specified as percentages, when added should give 100. Then the target values are assigned in specific numbers. This makes the contracting system more scientific and systematic. The criteria can be annually evaluated against the targets set and ascertained whether the enterprise has reached the expected level of performance.

The contract is signed between the Chief Executive of the PE and the Secretary of the administrative ministry. The PE has less power than the ministry, but at the same time, the it has more information regarding the technical and commercial questions of the sector in which the PE operates. The performance contract includes indicators relating to the business environment, industry structure (global and national level), price of the product, customer satisfaction, competition to the PE, the market position, the technological advances foreseen by the industry in the long run as well as short run. It is obvious, that the PE will have more information on all these aspects, which have relevance in day-to-day working of the enterprise. The ministry on the other hand will not have accessibility to all this information. Institutional arrangements, therefore, essentially call for a Performance Information System. This would allow necessary flow of information, which would be crucial both at the time of drawing the performance contracts as well as in the monitoring and evaluation process.

Reliable and accurate data are essential to the success of the entire system. The criteria adopted in contracts for evaluating the performance of the PE depends on the expectations of the government from the particular PE. The criteria, which are selected for the contracts, are an effort to specify only the return on investments. The performance contracting system should attempt to ensure that the performance contracting is finalised with clauses, which are fair to the PE and to the government.

MoU Mechanism

The MoU is an annual comprehensive document, which contains both the financial as well as the non-financial features of an enterprise. The document acts as an indicator of how the enterprise has faired on almost all the areas.

The formulation of MoU for a particular year starts with the Annual Plan. The targeting coincides with the annual planning of the enterprise. In the month of November, the PEs are supplied with guideline for the formulation of MoU by the Department of Public Enterprises (DPE). This acts as a framework on the basis of which the criteria is fixed and the targets are set. The heads of all the concerned departments of the enterprise, especially finance, commerce, corporate planning, management services together and decide upon the criteria for the year and what are the weightages to be attached to them. The Board of Directors (BoDs) then discuss the tentative framework, with the Chief Executive Officer (CEO) and the heads of the concerned departments. A decision is reached as to what are going to be the targets of the year from the enterprise side which have to be negotiated with the Government. The next important step is the negotiation process, the assumed targets are then negotiated with the government and the MoU is finalised for the year.

Based on these targets, the enterprises are evaluated at the end of the year. The process adopted for formalising an MoU involves the enterprise management, the administrative ministry and the DPE. MoU gives a complete picture as to how the enterprise is expected to perform and on what basis it is going to be evaluated. One of the drawbacks of the system is that during the process of negotiations there is ample scope for the parties on either side to adjust the target level in a way that it would ensure good performance.

Infrastructure for MoU in India

Design and implementation of the MoU system for the PEs in India is the responsibility of the DPE.

High Power Committee

At the apex of the framework is the High Power Committee (HPC). It is the overall in charge, chaired by the Cabinet Secretary and consisting of those Secretaries who do not sign the MoU themselves, but are concerned about the public sector. The HPC is a third party judge which evaluates the performance of PE in a fair manner.

The Inter-Ministry Standing Committee (IMSC)

The IMSC assists the HPC. The Secretary (Public Enterprises) chairs this committee. It consists of members from Planning Commission, Department of Economic Affairs, Department of Programme Implementation and the DPE. The IMSC screens the MoU at the first stage as soon as it is received by the Ad-hoc Task Force (ATF) for consideration by the HPC.

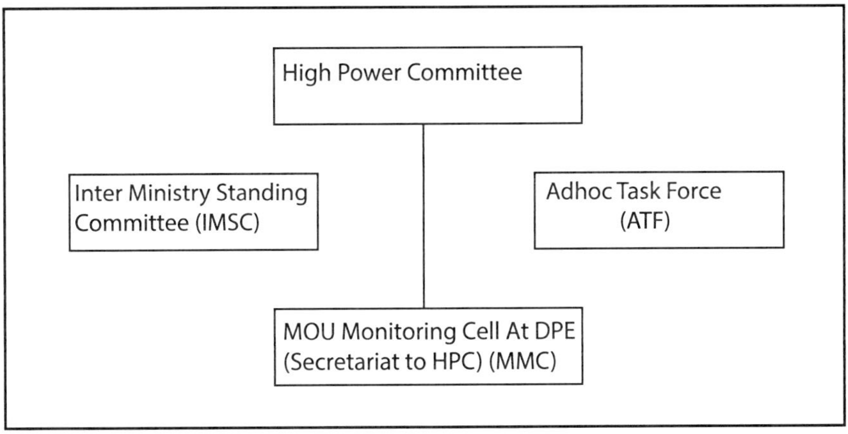

The Ad-hoc Task Force

The ATF is the body, which actually performs all the negotiations on targets and other important clauses. It consists of eminent management expects, ex-chief executives, chartered accountants, academicians, and economist. It is a body of experts who bring in high level of expertise and credibility to the whole system of MoU.

Task Force on MoU is a neutral and independent body of experts that assists the HPC on MoU and DPE in setting annual targets of CPSEs at the beginning of the year and performance evaluation of MoUs during and at the end of the year. In order to lend greater technical and professional expertise as well as diverse and rich experience to Task Force on MoU for the year 2011-12, CPSEs were categorised into 11 new syndicate groups including 2 newly created syndicate groups "Sick and Loss Making CPSEs" and "Section 25 CPSEs"; each syndicate normally having 6 members comprising 1 Convenor (senior most among the members), 1 administrative member (retired secretary to GoI), 1 finance expert/CA, 1 ex-CMD of any CPSE, 1 renowned academician, and 1 domain expert. There are 66 Task Force members and one Chairman as per the available data for the year 2011-12. The list of Task Force members (syndicate-wise) is available on *http://www.dpemou.nic.in*.

The Task Force commences negotiation meetings from January each year to evaluate and finalise the MoUs in respect of apex/holding CPSEs as well as subsidiary companies.

MoU-Monitoring Call (MMC)

The MoU monitoring cell is the nucleus of the whole contracting system. It is located at the DPE. All coordinating activities relating to the design, drafting, finalisation, monitoring and evaluation of the MoUs are undertaken by MMC.

Evaluation

Let us consider the example of evaluation of a public enterprise with the following performance:

i) Production 26,000.
ii) Profit 12 million currency units.
iii) Project Implementation 26 million currency units.

Criteria	*Unit*	*Weight*	*Score*		
			1.0	*0.8*	*0.25*
Production	Thousand (tonnes)	0.3	>>22	20	<<15
Profit	Million (currency units)	0.5	>>25	20	<<18
Project implementation	Million (currency units)	0.2	>>30	25	<<20

Box 4.1

Salient Features of MoU System in India

The system of MoU has been operational in India from the year 1989-1990 onwards. There are a number of factors that have come to light about the working of this system. There area few points that have been discussed below,

- The HPC, at the apex provides commitment at the higher level.
- The ATF, as a technical third party judge gives objectivity to the MoU evaluation.
- The presence of professionals and experts as members of ATF add to the professionalism to the evaluation system.
- The number of enterprises covered by MoU has come up to 109 in 1997-98 which makes the procedure highly reutilised. There is not enough time to concentrate on issues of concern.
- The absence of political commitment is seen as giving negative impact to the MoU system.
- Lack of proper incentive system at different levels of hierarchy is an important factor, which has not given a boost to the MoU system.

The scores will be calculated as:

i) If the actual production lies anywhere between 20,000 and 22,000 tonnes, the score will be only 0.8 (or 80%). Only when it exceeds 22,000 tonnes will the value jump to 1.00 (or 100%). In the above case, for production of 26,000 tonnes is above the score target for 1.0. Therefore, the score value is 1.0 x 0.3 (weightage) = 0.3.

ii) For profit, the score is 0.25 as the achievement is below the score target of 18 million for minimum score. The score value is 0.25 x 0.5 (weightage) = 0.125.

iii) For project implementation the score is 0.8 as the actual is between 250 and 300 million. The score value is 0.8 x 0.2 = 0.160.

iv) The composite score = 0.3 + 0.125 + 0.160 = 0.585. In other words the entire enterprise has obtained a total of 58.5 per cent marks in overall performance.

Conclusion

The institutional arrangements for implementing the system of MoU in India are very exhaustively designed and there are many checks and balances to ensure that enough thought process in involved during the design and roll out period. One of the key factors for successful implementation of the system is the need for a responsible BoDs, a trust worthy and efficient chief executive and other officials, and the most important is the attitude of the political authority who plays an important role in the whole exercise. All these factors taken into considerations help the contracts to go towards a successful completion of the MoU process. A HPC as the apex body supports the system of MoU in India and provides commitment at the higher level. The ATF, as a technical third party judge gives objectivity to the MoU evaluation. The presence of professionals and experts as the members of the ATF adds to the professional approach to the evaluation system. One of the key concerns have been the absence of political commitment, which is seen as giving negative impact to the MoU system. Lack of proper incentive system at different levels of hierarchy is an important factor, which has not given a boost to the MoU system in India.

References

Narain, Laxmi (1980). *Principles and Practice of Public Enterprise Management.* New Delhi: S. Chand & Company. p.22.

5

Performance Related Pay and MoU System

There have been numerous changes and refinements to the MoU system since its inception in the 1980s. The document is a performance management tool for monitoring and evaluating the performance of CPSEs (central public sector enterprises). The need for the MoU system was felt because of a lack of proper system for evaluating performance and setting goals and targets in the CPSEs. The enterprises, thus, lacked goal clarity, authority, transparency and accountability. The MoU system was essentially a system of MBO (management by objectives); a system that decreased political and bureaucratic interference and increased managerial autonomy and accountability.

The CPSEs in India have since their inception carried great importance in the larger scheme of the country's economy. The enterprises were envisioned to occupy the commanding heights of the economy and were to be an indispensable source of revenue for the government which would further use the revenue for solving the larger problems of the day such as poverty, starvation and healthcare. However, with the liberalisation and opening up of the economy, the CPSEs suddenly found themselves in intense competition with private companies and MNCs (multinational corporations). The resulting increase in opportunity and lucrative salaries offered in the private sector, led to many of the brightest talents which would have otherwise flocked to the public sector moving to the private sector.

One of the measures that allow the public sector companies to keep their edge over the private sector is the PRP (performance related pay). The PRP system links the performance of an individual employee with the incentives he/she receives, it is a system that is followed worldwide in all sectors for attracting new talent and also importantly, for retaining the exiting pool of talent. In this regard, the Second Pay Commission review committee for CPSEs in India, recommended the introduction of variable pay along with the fixed pay as an integral component of the compensation structure in CPSEs in India. The committee proposed to change the current pattern of compensation and bring in the component of variable pay with would supplement the basic pay which is already received by employees. The variable pay would depend on the position occupied by the employee in the company's hierarchy. The variable component would remain relatively low for lower level executives and progressively increase up the ranks to almost 200 per cent of the basic pay at the CEO level. The variable component is what is referred to as PRP and will be linked to individual, group, business-unit and company performance.

Performance Related Pay in Indian CPSEs

The incentives system is an integral part of the present system of MoU. The incentives system has two components: monetary and non-monetary incentives. These incentives combine to form part of the core aims and objectives of the system for CPSEs:

i) Increasing the autonomy of management of the company.

ii) Removing fuzziness in goals and objectives of the enterprises.

iv) To evaluate the performance of the managers in the public enterprises.

v) To provide incentives for better performance in the future.

The present system of incentives or PRP was conceptualised in the Second Pay Revision Committee report. According to the recommendations of the committee, the variable PRP would be available to the profit making CPSEs in accordance with their MoU rating. A 100 per cent eligibility for CPSEs achieving "excellent" rating, 80 per cent eligibility for rating of "very good", 60 per cent for "good" and 40 per cent for "fair" rating of basic pay. The CPSEs with "poor" rating for the MoU will not be eligible for PRP for that year.[1]

One of the important recommendations made by the committee is that it should be mandatory for all CPSEs to sign MoUs with their

1. *Public Enterprises Survey 2011-12 (http://dpe.nic.in/sites/upload_files/dpe/files/survey1112/survey01/vol1ch8.pdf)*

administrative ministries and secondly, it is also recommended that CPSEs not signing MoUs should not be eligible for PRP.

Prior to the introduction of the PRP system, CPSE employees had been paid the entire compensation which was guaranteed irrespective of the enterprise performance or individual performance. The earlier system was at odds with compensation in the private sector. In the private sector, a large portion of the compensation paid to individual employees has a variable component which is reflective of their contribution to the company's performance. The Second Pay Revision committee recommends that a similar system be introduced in the PSEs (public sector enterprises) as well. The variable component itself would vary at the different levels of management in the enterprises where the low level executives have a relatively low variable component which would increase as the individual moves higher up the hierarchy.[2]

Table 5.1

PRP as Percentage of Basic Pay

Grade	*A+, A and B Categories*	*C and D Categories*
E0 to E1	40	40
E2 to E3	40	40
E4 to E5	50	50
E6 to E7	60	60
E8 to E9	70	70
E10	100	—
Director	150	100
CMD	200	150

Source: Second Pay Revision Committee vide DPE OM No.2(70)/08-DPE (WC)-GL-XV/08 dtd. 26.11.2008 (*http://dpe.nic.in/sites/upload_files/dpe/files/Chapter_6_Recommendations_Final.pdf*)

The committee also makes recommendations regarding the PRP to individuals and groups based on their performance and need to develop a comprehensive Performance Management System (PMS). Since PRP to individuals and groups will be based on performance against key result areas, the Committee recommends that all CPSEs

2. Second Pay Revision Committee vide DPE OM No.2(70)/08-DPE (WC)-GL-XV/08 dtd. 26.11.2008 (*http://dpe.nic.in/sites/upload_files/dpe/files/Chapter_4_Paradigm%20Shift_Final.pdf*)

should develop a robust and transparent PMS system. CPSEs should adopt 'Bell curve approach' in grading the officers so that not more than 10 to 15 per cent executives are outstanding/excellent. Similarly 10 per cent of executives should be graded as below par.[3]

According to the committee, the PRP itself would be drawn from the Profit Before Tax (PBT) and the same would be linked to the individual, group, business unit and company performance. The determination of the amount of the variable payments would be linked to the MoU system in CPSEs and therefore it is recommended that the signing of MoU should be made mandatory for all CPSEs. The variable payments for companies as well as executives would be determined conditional on achieving pre-determined physical as well as financial targets. The companies would have to internalise the MoU process upto the lowest operative level.[4]

The PRP would come out of the profits of the company based on physical and financial performance in accordance with the methodology suggested by the committee, where 60 per cent of the performance pay would be given with a ceiling of 3 per cent PBT and 40 per cent of PRP would come out of 10 per cent of the incremental profit. And the total PRP would be limited to 5 per cent of the year's PBT. The committee recommends that for individual levels of PRP, the methodology can be finalised by the CPSE concerned. It is suggested that the enterprises put in place a rational and transparent PMS internally which would be decided by the CPSE. BSCs (balanced score cards) would also have to be introduced to determine the eligibility of PRP for each executive.[5]

Effective from 9 February 2009 a circular was issued by the Department of Public Enterprises (DPE) informing CPSEs to follow

---

3. Second Pay Revision Committee vide DPE OM No. 2(70)/08-DPE (WC)-GL-XV/08 dtd. 26.11.2008 *(http://dpe.nic.in/sites/upload_files/dpe/files/Chapter_6_Recommendations_Final.pdf)*

4. Second Pay Revision Committee vide DPE OM No. 2(70)/08-DPE (WC)-GL-XV/08 dtd. 26.11.2008 *(http://dpe.nic.in/sites/upload_files/dpe/files/Chapter_4_Paradigm%20Shift_Final.pdf)*

5. Second Pay Revision Committee vide DPE OM No. 2(70)/08-DPE (WC)-GL-XV/08 dtd. 26.11.2008 *(http://dpe.nic.in/sites/upload_files/dpe/files/Chapter_6_Recommendations_Final.pdf)*

the recommendation and methodology as suggested by the Second Pay Revision Committee report regarding the PRP.[6]

Case Study: Bharat Heavy Electronics Ltd. (BHEL)[7]

BHEL is a Maharatna Company and has been a profit making SOE (state-owned enterprise) since 1971-72 and is a major integrated power plant equipment manufacturer in the world. In BHEL, a cascading process is used to ensure that the targets set in the MoU filters down to the lowest levels in the company and thus the targets are achieved throughout the company in a uniform manner. BHEL achieves this through company BSC which is cascaded to all constituent divisions of the company to ensure that the relevant parameters of the MoU are included in their respective BSCs. Subsequently, individual performance plans are prepared based on the BSCs thereby ensuring MoU targets are cascaded to working levels.

BHEL has also been implementing PRP (performance related pay). PRP is the incentive system which is attached to the MoU system where the performance rating received by the company in the MoU cycle determines the bonus that accrues to the individual employees of the company. The individual performance ratings are assigned based on 'bell curve' approach. The scheme is applicable to executives and a section of the supervisors in the company. The workers of the company are however not included in the scheme of PRP and their incentives are settled through collective bargaining.

The quantum of incentives received by the managers of the company is dependent on two factors:

i) MoU rating: The rating the company receives in the MoU determines the quantum of incentives; higher the rating in the MoU, higher the incentives.

ii) Individual Performance Rating: This is based on individual

6. Via the "Revision of Pay Scales of Executives of Central Public Enterprises (CPSEs)" w.e.f 01.01.2007; "Performance Management System (PMS): Linkage of Performance Related Pay (PRP) with MoU Rating of CPSEs and Performance of Individual Executives" vide OM No. 2(70)/08-DPE (WC)-GL IV/09

7. Presentation made by Mr B.P. Rao, CMD, Bharat Heavy Electronics Limited, at the international workshop on *Performance Evaluation and Management of State Owned Enterprises*, January 2015, New Delhi.

performance against targets, many of which are derived from MoU targets.

Challenges in the Implementation of the Incentive Scheme

i) Implementation of Bell Curve approach: It often becomes difficult to differentiate between contribution of individuals in team operation, which is very critical in a company like BHEL. Thus in order to implement a Bell Curve approach based on individual performance requires forced distribution which leads to adverse impact on the team work.

ii) Differing criteria to decide incentive payments: The PRP is applicable to the enterprise managers which includes executives and senior supervisors, while the workers of the company are wholly excluded from the PRP scheme and they receive their incentive payments through collective bargaining. This creates an unhealthy situation where the incentives for different levels of management do not adhere to the uniform scheme of receiving incentive payments.

iii) MoU target setting process: Another challenge that is faced by BHEL is the ever increasing MoU targets irrespective of the economic atmosphere or conditions in which the PSU has to operate.

All of the factor mentioned afore have a direct impact on the MoU ratings and thus on the incentive scheme, though the enterprise managers have no control over the external factors affecting the MoU ratings.

Case Study: Hindustan Petrochemicals Limited (HPCL)[8]

HPCL is another CPSE that has internally integrated the MoU system with their PMS. The company starts the process by first finalising the vision, mission and objectives at the beginning of the year; new strategic areas for growth and profitability are also identified.

8. Presentation made by Shri Nishi Vasudeva,C&MD,HPCL at the international workshop on 'Performance Evaluation and Management of State Owned Enterprises',January 2015,New Delhi.

Then at the director level, MoAs (Memorandum of Agreements) are agreed upon with SBUs (strategic business units) which translates into the annual plan and at the bottom of the ladder that is the field level . An AOP (annual operating plan) is formulated and score cards (L1-L4) are used to measure performance.

The company also has KPI (key performance indicators) which area combination of parameters and composite Score. In terms of CPSE, the incentives are of two types: (i) monetary incentives: PRP based on MoU performance and (ii) non-monetary incentives: MoU excellence awards. As for the employees: (i) monetary incentives include PRP linked to employee performance against MoU based on KPIs and (ii) non-monetary performance includes recognition through employee awards such as HP icon, outstanding achiever, HP Gaurav.

Conclusion

With the liberalisation and opening up of the economy, the CPSEs suddenly found themselves in intense competition with private companies and MNCs. The resulting increase in opportunity and lucrative salaries offered in the private sector, many of the brightest talents which would have otherwise flocked to the public sector were now moving to the private sector. It is observed that one of the measures that allow the public sector companies to keep their edge over the private sector is the PRP. This system has been adopted worldwide in all sectors for attracting new talent and also importantly, retaining the exiting pool of talent.

6

Results Framework Management System-MoU (RFMS-MoU)

Introduction

The Memorandum of Understanding (MoU) is a negotiated document between the Government, acting as the owner of CPSE (centre public sector enterprise) and the corporate management of the CPSE. It contains the intentions, obligations and mutual responsibilities of the Government and the CPSE, and is directed towards strengthening CPSE management by expressing a convergence of will between the parties, indicating an intended common line of action. It seeks to address three basic questions: (i) What are Public Enterprise's main objectives for the year? (ii) What actions are proposed to achieve these objectives? and (iii) How to assess the degree of progress made in implementing these actions? That is, what are the relevant criterion and their targets?

The beginnings of the MoU system in India can be traced to the recommendation made by the Arjun Sengupta Committee on Public Enterprises in 1984. During the initial years of MoU implementation, Government of India laid greater emphasis on the core sectors like steel, heavy engineering, coal, power, petroleum and fertilisers. In the year 1987-88, a pilot run of the MoU system was carried out with four enterprises. Over the years, the number of CPSE under the ambit of the MoU has increased exponentially. Today over 250 CPSEs (including subsidiaries and CPSEs under various stages of construction) have been brought into the ambit of the MoU system. During this period, considerable modifications and improvements in the structure of and procedures for preparing and finalising the MoUs have been made. These changes have been brought about on the basis of experiences in the working of the MoU system and supported by studies carried out by experts on specific aspects of the MoU system from time to time.

Figure 6.1

Contribution of CPSEs to National Exchequer (in crore)

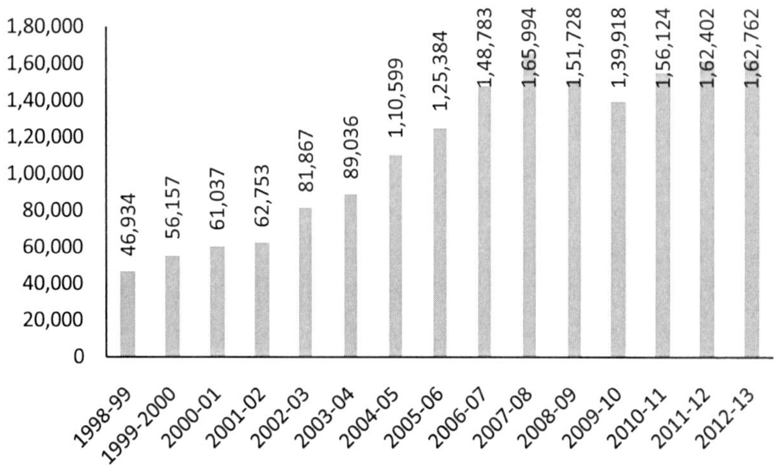

Source: A Study on Public Sector Enterprises Transformation, Competitiveness & Sustainability by KPMG.

Figure 6.2

The Impact of MoU System

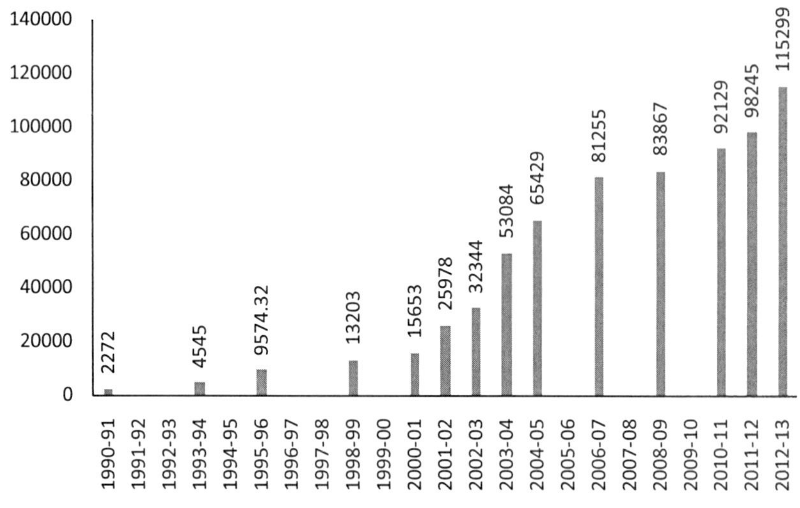

Source: The Public Enterprise Survey 1991-2012, Department of Public Enterprise, Government of India.

The major reasons for the survival of the MoU system over the years can be attributed to the vast impact it has had on the performance of the PEs (public enterprises), e.g., the dramatic and relatively steady impact of the MoU system on parameters such as surplus generated for the exchequer, increase in net profit, etc.

The RFMS-MoU has been developed by Department of Public Enterprises (DPE), Government of India (GoI) and Institute of Public Enterprise (IPE), Hyderabad, as a tool to strengthen the system of MoU in India. This initiative has been taken under the GOPEMPAL Project (Government Performance Management and Peer Assisted Learning Project.[1]

About Results Framework Management System (RFMS)

The RFMS is a web-based system, originally designed for the online preparation of the RFD (results framework document). RFD is a performance contract documenting the understanding between a Minister (GoI) representing the people's mandate, and the Secretary (GoI) of the Department responsible for implementing this mandate. Thus, the RFMS is designed and mapped on the basis of the guidelines issued by the Performance Management Division (PMD), Cabinet Secretariat, Government of India.

The RFMS is developed by the National Informatics Centre (NIC) under the guidance of the PMD, Cabinet Secretariat. As this is a web application, the only basic requirement at the user end is: (i) a computer and (ii) internet connectivity. The system is technology neutral, built on open source platforms, compatible with all browsers and has strong authentication and authorisation to prevent sensitive government data from getting leaked, making it extremely safe, user friendly and convenient. Another interesting feature of RFMS is that it can be used for both evaluating and monitoring. The user can feed in monthly achievement for monitoring their progress and/or compute a composite score at the end of the year to evaluate their performance. Focused on 'Managerial Performance', it provides a unified, and single view of performance.

1. The authors are thankful to the contributors Mr Ritvik Mishra and Ms Shreya Dutt who have been associated with the development of this tool.

As of 2014, 80 Government Departments/Ministries along with 800 Responsibility Centers (subordinate offices) are using this software to prepare their RFDs every year making it one of the most popularly used software by the Indian government today. State governments of Assam, Kerala, Haryana, are also using the RFMS to prepare their RFDs.

Need for RFMS

The basic reason for the development of a web-based system for the preparation of an RFD was to ensure consistency, transparency and accountability amongst users. This became even more significant with the increase in the target population using the software. The system provides a generic platform to all the departments, ministries and their subordinate offices for preparing their RFDs in a common format, hence when these documents are sent to the Cabinet Secretariat for evaluation they are in the same format making the criteria for evaluation and understanding generic.

RFMS-MoU

In case of MoUs, the last e-development (electronic development) which took place was preparation of the MoU using the excel format, which happened in the early-mid 1990s. Since then, no substantive measures have been taken to develop a generic e-platform. Furthermore, a cursory glance at MoUs of different CPSEs revealed inconsistencies in adhering to the guidelines. This was also highlighted in the Mankad Committee Report (2012) which not only states that there was a need to ensure "...uniformity in approach...minimize the element of subjectivity in the selection of options..." Hence, like RFDs, it was observed that there is a need to make MoU on software which is generic and consistent for all the CPSEs signing MoU. The committee also noted that there is a need for "better harmony, synchronization and synergies between the two systems (MoU and RFD system), whose ultimate objectives are similar".

When one examines and compares the MoU prepared by different CPSEs it is startling to know that though they address the same three basic questions (mentioned above) but the way these questions are addressed differ. For example, the criteria value that can be given in an RFD has to be either number or a date hence maintaining consistency amongst different department, whereas in case of a CPSE, criteria value could be other than numbers and date. Excerpts from a signed MoU is shown as an example in Table 6.1.

Table 6.1

Variation in the Unit of Criteria in MoUs

Parameter	*Criterion*	*Unit*	*Marks*	*Exellent*	*Very Good*	*Good*	*Fair*	*Poor*
The degree of success in implementing the CSR and Sustainbility projects undertaken during the year	Bio-diversity conservation and CO_2 sequestration at Bolani Mine	Activity	0.50	Plantation of forest trees	Plantation of fruit trees	stream restoration	Grass land productivity assessment	Ground water recharging measurements

Criterion	*Unit*	*WTS*	*Excellent*	*Very Good*	*Good*	*Fair*	*Poor*
Manpower Rationalisation: Achieving Closing Manpower as Per HRP 2013-14	Manpower	1	Manpower Equal to/ less than planned closing	Manpower 1000 more than planned closing	Manpower 2000 more than planned closing	Manpower 2500 more than planned closing	Manpower 3000 more than planned closing

One can infer from Table 6.1 that that in the absence of a proper e-system it is difficult to maintain consistency amongst MoUs of various CPSEs. Thus, keeping in view the above mentioned issues, it was decided that rather than building a new software, an already existing software can be molded to fit the requirements of the MoU system as well. Furthermore, with an intention to build harmony between the MoU and the RFD system as suggested by the Mankad Committee, it was decided that the RFMS system should be used to make MoU.

Objectives of RFMS-MoU

i) Mandatory objectives: This is a new concept borrowed from the RFD system. They are objectives which are approved by the High Power Committee (HPC) on MoU and are applicable to all

CPSEs. Their criterions, its weights and its targets will also be fixed by the HPC and would be common to all. In the RFMS-MoU system, they appear in the light-pink field.

ii) User defined objectives: These are objectives that may be specific to the organisation. The user can add as many objectives as they like by clicking on the "add new" button at the bottom of the page. Once they are entered in the system, they would appear in the white coloured field.

iii) Partially mandatory objectives: Unlike RFMS-RFD, RFMS-MoU has a set of 'partially mandatory' objectives which are objectives that are common to all CPSEs but their weights, criteria, etc., are defined by the user or the category if CPSE as mentioned in the DPE guidelines for MoU. For example, 'Sound Financial Management' is an objective that is common to all CPSEs but its weightage depends on the whether it is a loss-making (weightage=40) or profit making (weightage=50). These objectives appear in yellow coloured fields in the system. Table 6.2 shows the list of Partially Mandatory Objectives as given in the RFMS-MoU.

Table 6.2

Partially Mandatory Objectives in RFMS-MoU and its Relation to the Objectives in Paper-based MoU

	Partially Mandatory Objectives in RFMS-MoU	*Corresponding Parameters in Paper-based MoU*
1	Sound Financial Management.	All Financial indicators and parameters
2	Sound Physical Performance	Initiatives for Growth (IG), Productivity and Internal Processes (PIP), Technology Quality and Innovative Parameters (TQIP), Sector/Enterprise Specific Parameters
3	Contribution to Social Welfare	Corporate Social Responsibility
4	Ensuring Sustainable Development	Sustainability
5	Enhancing Reseach and Development	Research and Development
6	Improving Human Resource Management	Human Resource management
7	Improving Corporate Governance	Corporate Governance (currently with negative marking in MoU)
8	Effective Project Implementation	Project Management and Implementation

How Does RFMS-MoU Work: Details of the Steps/Stages

The RFMS-MoU is broadly divided into six sections. Each section corresponds to a particular section in the existing paper-based MoU. Table 6.3 gives a brief description of the six sections in the RFMS-MoU and its corresponding segment in the paper-based MoU. One major addition to the existing MoU structure is the introduction of Section 6 in RFMS-MoU. The concept of this section is borrowed from the RFD system. This section urges CPSEs to think about the outcome/ impact of the objectives that they are working towards.

Table 6.3

Sections of the RFMS-MoU and the Corresponding Sections of Paper-based MoU

	Sections of the RFMS-MoU	*Corresponding Sections of Paper-based MoU*
Section 1	Department's Vision, Mission, Objectives and Functions.	Part 1.
Section 2	Inter se priorities among key objectives, success indicators and targets.	Part 2.
Section 3	Trend values of the success indicators.	Past year Data in part 2/ Annexure-VI.
Section 4	Description and definition of success indicators and proposed measurement methodology.	Annexure/Footnotes of MoU.
Section 5	Specific performance requirements from other departments that are critical for delivering agreed results.	Part 3- Commitments/Assistance from the Government.
Section 6	Outcome/Impact of activities of department	To be Developed.
	Uploading of documents (in Section 2 and Section 4)	Annexure VII and VIII.

Section 1: Vision, Mission, Function and Objectives

Section 1 of the RFMS-MoU entails the vision, mission, function and objectives. Vision, in short, may be defined as 'what' the CPSE wants to be in the long-run and is typically generic and grand. The mission statement is the nuts and bolts of the vision. Mission is the 'who, how and why' of the vision. Function is related to what the CPSE is legally required to do—usually mentioned in the 'Memorandum of Association'; only the core functions should be mentioned here to give an idea about the organisation. Objectives represent the requirements to be achieved by the CPSE in a particular sector by a selected set of policies and programmes over a specific period of time (short, medium, long). Generally, objectives are classified into two types: (i) outcome objectives which address ends to achieve, and (ii) process objectives which specify the means to achieve the objectives. As far as possible,the CPSEs should focus on outcome objectives. This outcome-orientedness is reiterated in section 6 which has been discussed later in the paper.

An interesting fact about the RFMS-MoU is that, it is mapped in a way that sections are interlinked. An input in a particular section has subsequent relations with the following sections. This concept mirrors the underline concept of the MoU that each section should flow from one another—the mission flows from the vision and the mission determines the objectives that the organisation needs to achieve in order to complete the mission. The RFMS-MoU is also made to reflect similar interlinkages. For example, the system requires the user to define the objectives only once in section 1, they are automatically reflected in the subsequent sections 2, 3 and 6; criteria mentioned in section 2 will automatically reflect in sections 3, 4 and 5. To explain this further, all criteria defined in section 2 are available for selection by users in section 5 (Dependency).

Section 2: Inter se Priorities Among Key Objectives, Success Indicators and Targets

Section 2 is the heart of the MoU as it captures the essence of what the CPSE plans to achieve in the said year. It enlists the objectives of the CPSE, the 'actions' it proposes to take to achieve the said objectives, 'criterions' which specify how the progress would be measured and the 'targets'. Even though in both the formats—paper-based MoU and the RFMS-MoU—the targets are set on a 5-point scale, the one minor difference is that, in RFMS-MoU is on a 100 point scale. Table 6.4 gives the 6 columns that form this section.

Section 3: Trend Value

Section 3 in the RFMS-MoU corresponds to Annex IV in the paper-based MoU. It talks about the trend values of the criterions. For every criteria, the software allows the CPSEs to provide data for the past 5 years, projected values for the future two years and target value for the current year. The target value for the current year is automatically taken from the 'very good' column of the criteria value in section 2 (as shown in the Table 6.4). Assuming that the user is preparing the MoU for the year 2013-14, often it is asked, "does this section have to be complete?","Can we leave some fields blank?" Yes, an user can leave the fields blank; if an action is being initiated in the current year, then no values would be listed in the previous year column. Also, in case an action is going to be completed in the current year, then no values would be listed in the next 2 years. Section 2 figures are not to be copies here and care should be taken that the date values are for the relevant year listed in the column. For the composition of section 3, please refer to Table 6.5.

Table 6.4

Columns Composting Section 2 of RFMS-MoU

Column 1	*Column 2*	*Column 3*	*Column 4*	*Column 5*	*Column 6*					
Objective	*Weight of Objective*	*Actions*	*Success Indicator*	*Unit*	*Weight of Success Indicator*	*Target/Criteria Value*				
						Excellent	*Very Good*	*Good*	*Fair*	*Poor*
						100%	*90%*	*80%*	*70%*	*60%*
Objective 1		Action 1								
		Action 2								
		Action 3								
Objective 2		Action 1								
		Action 2								
		Action 3								
Objective 3		Action 1								
		Action 2								
		Action 3								

Table 6.5

Composition of Section 3

Objective	*Actions*	*Criterion*	*Unit*	*Actual Value for FY 2009/10*	*Actual Value for FY 2010/11*	*Actual Value for FY 2011/12*	*Actual Value for FY 2012/13*	*Actual Value for FY 2013/14 (anticipated)*	*Target Value for FY 2014/15*	*Projected Value for FY 2015/16*	*Projected Value for FY 16/17*
1	1										
	2										
	3										
2	1										
	2										
	3										

Section 4: Description and Definition of Success Indicators and Proposed Measurement Methodology

Section 4 in the RFMS-MoU allows the CPSEs to give detailed definitions of various criterions mentioned in Section 2 and their proposed measurement methodology. Wherever required, the rationale for using the proposed criterion can be provided by the CPSE in this section. This section also gives users an option to upload any document in support of the specific criterion.

Table 6.6

Composition of Section 4

SI. No.	*Criertion*	*Description*	*Definition*	*Measurement*	*General Comments*

Section 5: Dependency

Section 5 in the RFMS-MoU corresponds to Annexure 3 used in the present Paper-based MoU system. This section aims to elicit the dependency that a CPSE may have on any other organisation. The CPSE is required to claim the dependency on other Departments/ Ministries/Organisation based on the format mentioned in Table 6.7:

Table 6.7

Composition of Section 5

Location Type	*State*	*Organisation Type*	*Organisation Name*	*Relevant Criterion*	*What is your requirement from this organisation*	*Justification for this requirement*	*Please quantify your requirement from this organissation*	*What happens if your requirement is not met*

By choosing this option department has to enter specific performance requirements from other departments that are critical for delivering agreed results. Another interesting feature of the RFMS

MoU that it allowas a detailed printable report of Section 5. A CPSE can not only see the dependency it has claimed on other departments/ministries/PSUs in the system, the dependency claimed by other departments/ministries/PSUs from their organisation can also be seen.

Section 6: Outcome/Impact

This section contains the broad outcomes and the expected impact the CPSE has on national welfare. It aims to capture the very purpose for which the CPSE exists. This section has been added to the MoU system for information only and to keep reminding us about not only the purpose of the existence of the CPSE but also the rationale for undertaking the MoU exercise. However, the year-end evaluation is done only against the targets mentioned in Section 2. The whole point of MoU is to ensure that the CPSE serves the purpose for which they were created in the first place.

Table 6.8

Composition of Section 6

S. No	*Outcome / Impact*	*Jointly responsible for influencing this outcome/impact with the following organisation (s) / departments/ ministry(ies)*	*Criterion*	*Unit*	*2012-13*	*2013-14*	*2014-15*	*2015-16*	*2016-17*

As can be seen from the above, the RFMS-MoU is not a new concept. It has been introduced to codify the existing MoU system and to introduce uniformity and consistency amongst the MoU practitioners.

Current Status of RFMS MoU

The first OM (official memo) on this subject, informing CPSEs about the introduction of RFMS-MoU was issued on March 18, 2014 by DPE, Government of India. The training on RFMS-MoU has been underway since March 2014. Since then, around 240 officials from 116 CPSEs have been trained on RFMS-MoU.[2]

Currently, the RFMS-MoU is on a trial run. DPE has instructed all CPSEs to enter the 2013-14 data (already signed MoUs) on the RFMS. This exercise is aimed at basically testing the software. Thus, the users' feedback and suggestions are most crucial at this stage.

Each person who has been trained in the RFMS has also been made a part of a virtual COP (community of practice) on RFMS-MoU. This COP can be accessed through: *www.gopempal.org*. This is a very active community of practitioners of RFMS-MoU. The community is also an innovative way to resolve issues being faced by users. Over and above the COP, helpdesk services are also being provided to all the users.

Benefits of RFMS-MoU

The major benefits that introduction of RFMS-MoU, based on the MoU guidelines issued by DPE, aims to bring about are:

i) RFMS facilitates CPSEs to prepare MoU online and input achievements.

ii) Access to RFMS MoU is restricted to officials nominated by CPSEs and is granted through highly secured User Id/Password

iii) The 'user ids' are mapped with the organisational details such as kind of the organisation (Maharatna, Miniratna, Section 25 company, loss making, etc.) in a way that it reflects the parameters pertaining to an organisation as set by the DPE guidelines. For example, for sick and loss making company the weight assigned to financial parameter by DPE is 40. When a sick and loss making organisation keys in their 'user id' in RFMS, the weight for such parameters will automatically reflect as what DPE has defined in the MoU guidelines.

iii) The CPSEs can take out prints, save and send electronic copy of the MoU they have prepared. The RFMS-MoU provides output in PDF as well as excel formats. The CPSE can also see and take a printed copy of the dependency they have claimed on other

2. More information on the RFMS training can be found on *www.performance.gov.in*.

organisations, ministry as well as the dependency others have claimed on their organisation.

iv) Online availability of previous years MoU achievements/ composite scores/trend values to the CPSE and DPE.

Reference

Arjun Sengupta Committee Report (1986). *Report on Policy for Public Enterprises.*

Department of Public Enterprises (2014). *Memorandum of Understanding Guidelines 2014-15.* Government of India. Available from: *http://www.dpeMoU.nic.in/MoUFiles/MoU2014-15.pdf*

Department of Public Enterprises and Performance Management Division (2014). *Results Framework Management System Software.* Performance Management Division, Cabinet Secretariat, Government of India. Available from: *www.rfmstraining.nic.in*

Government of India (2008). *Report of the Working Group on Review of MoU Guidelines in CPSEs* (Chairman: Ashok Chandra).

Mankad Committee Report (2012). *Report of the Committee on the MoU System, 2012.*

Performance Management Division (2014). *Memorandum of Understanding.* Available from: *http://www.performance.gov.in/?q=MoU*

———. (2014). *Results Framework Document Guidelines 2014-15.* Cabinet Secretariat, Government of India. Available from: *www.performance.gov.in/?q=rfd-guidelines*

———. (2014a). *Results Framework Management System Hands-on Training Material.* Cabinet Secretariat, Government of India

———. (2014b). *Results Framework Management System Hands-on Training Presentations.* Cabinet Secretariat, Government of India.

Powell, S. (2004) "The Challenges of Performance Measurement", *Management Decision* 42(8): 1017-23.

UNDP (2014). *Proceedings of the Global Roundtable on Government Performance Management.*

7

MoU System in India

An In-depth Analysis

In order to get a first hand feel of the issues and challenges in the implementation of MoU system in India, a semi-structured questionnaire (Annexure A-2) was developed for the following stakeholders involved in the process of implementation of the MoU System:

i) CMDs/Managers of CPSEs (Central Public Sector Enterprises).

ii) The administrative ministry.

iii) The Task Force members.

The questionnaire was sent to all the CPSEs which signed MoUs for the year 2013-14 and the syndicate members of the Ad-hoc Task Force (ATF) formed by Government of India for the review of MoU. Responses were received from only 15 enterprises and 3 Task Force members in hard and soft copy format. The enterprises that responded include miniratna, navaratna, sick Companies under Board for Industrial and Financial Reconstruction (BIFR) (See Annexure A-1).

Based on the responses received from the stakeholder,the key concerns on the implementation of the MoU system have emerged:

Key Concerns of the CPSEs

i) Uniform MoU formats have been prescribed for all enterprises. Need to develop specific formats for CPSEs (trading, commercial, service, manufacturing etc). However, it has to be done within the standard framework and guidelines prescribed by the government.

ii) Formats are lengthy and complex and there is a need to simplify them.

iii) MoU guidelines should not be amended every year. Some

enterprises highlighted the need for sufficient time lag between issuance of the guidelines and submission of draft MoU.

iv) The MoU parameters must be more enterprise specific. Production, sales and margin related financial and quantitative parameters should be fixed scientifically taking into consideration prevailing conditions instead of just taking an increase of 5-10 per cent blanket increase in yearly targets.

v) The MoU system is too dependent on financial parameters. Need to focus on process—e.g., projects, technology, R&D. Innovation should be given higher priority in MoU as the success of an enterprise depends on these elements.

vi) Benchmarking is a very important activity that should be taken up on a continuous basis. Through some enterprises like MOIL Limited said that they take up a benchmarking exercise with national and international players, many others said that they do not follow any such activity. In order to make the MoU system more meaningful and to set competitive targets, maharatnas/navratnas should be benchmarked with the Asian best as well as the global best apart from the private and public sector companies with whom they compete in India.

vii) Enterprises stressed the need for more functional autonomy for achieving the targets under MoU.

viii) Obligation of Government towards the enterprise must also be assessed and how they have fulfilled their commitments is a critical element to evaluate.

ix) The approach to MoU has been based on the Balanced Score Card philosophy,therefore it must focus on financial perspective, customer perspective, internal process perspective and learning and growth perspective. Only then will it become a holistic approach to measuring performance and enhancing efficiency in enterprises.

x) The PRP system needs to be further streamlined. The Bell Curve model which has to be mandatorily followed creates a lot of dissatisfaction among the employees and marginalises people by 10-15 per cent each year. Instead of being a motivational tool, it works towards building mistrust among employees.

Some of the key themes that were covered in the questionnaire are analysed and dpresented below.

Number of CPSEs Signing MoU

Out of the 15 respondents a majority of the enterprises (6) have been entering into MoUs since 1991-92 (23 years) while 4 have been signing MoUs for less than a decade, the rest 11 enterprises have been signing since 2 decades or more. This suggests that the MoU system has been thoroughly internalised in these CPSEs and has become a permanent fixture in the operation of the enterprises across the board, be it navaratna, miniratna or sick enterprises.

Table 7.1

Year of Signing MoUs

S No	*No of Respon-dents*	*1986-2013 (28 years)*	*1989-2013 (25 years)*	*1990-2013 (24 years)*	*1991-2013 (23 years)*	*1992-2013 (22 years)*	*2005-2013 (8 years)*	*2006-2013 (7 years)*	*2007-2013 (6 years)*
1	15	1	1	2	6	1	2	0	2

When compared to a similar study done by Mishra and Potaraju (1999-2000), it reveals that not only has the number of enterprises signing MoU has gone up since then, but also that many of the enterprises have persevered with the MoU process.

Rating in MoUs

With the introduction of the MoU system, a scientific evaluation method was adopted for the PES (public enterprises) wherein they are evaluated at the end of the year, based on the pre-set targets. The scores are then placed on a five point Rating Scale. The scores ranging from 1-1.5 are rated as 'Excellent', between 1.5 and 2 as 'Very Good', between 2.5 and 3 as 'Good', between 3.5 and 4 as 'Average', and between 4.5 and 5 as 'fair'.

Enterprises were asked the rating and scores that they had obtained for the last 10 years subject to their signing the MoUs. As already mentioned, the majority of the respondents have signed the MoUs well before a decade.

Almost all the respondents who sent back the questionnaires have scored excellent or very good ratings for all the years they have been signing the MoU. This also shows that enterprises with good performance under MoU were motivated enough to respond to the questionnaire while the others did not.

Planning Process in CPSEs

On asked about the various methods of planning process in the enterprise, the respondents said that they had a system of developing a corporate plan, annual CAPEX plan, resource plan, risk management plan etc. On being asked how the enterprises align the MoU plan with the planning process, most of them said that the MoU targets are set keeping in mind the major plans like corporate plan, RFD and other strategic plans, and production plan and the MoU targets are aligned with their planning process as a whole.

Financial Delegation

On asked whether the financial delegation of powers to CPSEs facilitated the enterprise to take investment decisions in a faster and smoother manner, they responded that financial delegation is an important step towards greater autonomy for managers in the enterprises. CPSEs generally have a lot of constraints when it comes to taking financial decisions as they are accountable to multiple principals and expected to fulfil multiple objectives. They are bound by the decisions of the administrative ministry, the Planning Commission, the finance ministry and other funding organisations like World Bank, etc. This usually hinders the financial autonomy of the enterprises. One of the functions of the MoU is to afford greater freedom to the managers to take financial decisions and so it is a pertinent question for enterprises signing the MoU.

Out of the 15 respondents, 13 of the enterprises answered in the affirmative that the financial delegation of powers to CPSEs has facilitated the enterprises to take their investment decisions in a faster and smoother way. One enterprise, Mumbai Railway Vikas Corporation Ltd. (MRVC), responded that the company does not invest in any adventures except parking surplus funds temporarily in the banks as per Department of Public Enterprises' (DPE) guidelines and so the question does not apply to them.

Table 7.2

Financial Delegation

Respondents	*Yes*	*No*	*No Answer*
15	13	0	2

MoU and Accountability of CPSEs

On being asked if MoU has helped the enterprise secure greater accountability at the various levels, respondents said that they see accountability as a major component of any performance management tool and CPSEs being public companies have to be made accountable for every decision they undertake and MoU seeks to bolster that belief through target setting and ensuring that the different departments are doing what is expected of them.

The problem of public accountability comprises control of the PEs directly by the parliament and indirectly through the minister concerned, and also making the management responsible and answerable to the minister and through him to the parliament. The parliamentary objective of accountability is to define the relationship between various authorities so as to focus on responsibility, facilitate coordination with related programmes, ensure consistency in the implementation of the policy by the government, conduct operations with maximum efficiency and economy, and in accordance with the law. It would further produce information to enable appropriate authorities to evaluate the effectiveness of the operations and from time to time apply pressures and sanctions to remove inertia and obstacles in the way of fulfilling the objectives.

Accountability is an essential feature of all forms of democratic governments. It refers to the fact that each person who is given authority must recognise the fact that the executive above him will judge the quality of his performance. PEs are the creation of the government and are placed in the hands of Board of Directors (BoDs) for implementation of the development and industrial tasks envisaged by the government. In the case of the private sector, shareholders are the owners and the accountability of the managers is to ensure profits for them.

Rationale of Public Accountability

The PSEs do involve complete separation between ownership and management, which results in the absence of any control or vigilance by the shareholders. The management is placed in the hands of people who have no stake in the enterprises they manage. This gives rise to a need for putting such enterprises under some suitable control and making the management responsible and answerable to some authority and that being the parliament.

The question of enhanced accountability through the MoU was asked and out of the 15 respondents, 13 respondents answered in the affirmative, confirming that the MoU system enhances the accountability in CPSEs internally. One enterprise answered in the negative and one enterprise did not answer the question.

One of the enterprises informed that based on the MoU targets, internal targets are set for various financial and non-financial parameters and are assigned to different departments, paving the way for enhanced accountability at various levels.

Another respondent explained that the MoU helps in laying the targets for the individual component of the project which makes everyone aware in the organisation and strive to achieve those targets. It also helps in getting the commitment for providing the resources from the administrative ministry. The last part of the response is significant because the MoU focuses on ensuring the accountability of the CPSEs and usually the administrative ministries are not made accountable for their end of the MoU commitments. If the administrative ministry is made to keeping their commitments due to the MoU document, it is an important aspect of the instrument.

In a similar study conducted by Mishra and Potaraju (1999-2000), 76 enterprises answered the question whether the MoU system has increased accountability. Out of the 76 enterprises, 40 per cent of the enterprises felt that the accountability was enhanced, another 40 per cent felt the opposite, while the rest felt that accountability was enhanced partially. This has changed over the intervening time.

Table 7.3

Greater Accountability

Respondents	*Yes*	*No*	*No answer*
15	13	1	1

Enhanced Commitment

On being asked whether the MoU system helped your enterprise to increase commitment to various departments and individuals, out of the 15 respondents who answered the question, all the enterprises answered that the MoU system has indeed helped them increase commitment to various departments and individuals.

Table 7.4

Increased Commitment

Respondents	*Yes*	*No*	*No Answer*
15	14	0	1

Technical Expertise for MoU

On being asked if there is any technical expertise drawn from outside to take up this activity, the CPSEs said that technical expertise is a very important aspect of target setting and evaluation process of MoU. Expertise drawn from outside could help further fine tune the financial targets and non-financial targets.

With the exception of NMDC, which did not answer the question, the rest of the 14 enterprises did not draw technical expertise in the MoU process.

Table 7.5

Expertise from Outside

Respondents	*Yes*	*No*	*No Answer*
15	0	14	1

Benchmarking Performance

Does the enterprise conduct benchmarking exercise with similar companies in India?

Does the enterprise conduct benchmarking exercise with companies around the globe?

Out of the 15 respondents who answered the questionnaire, 10 enterprises did not conduct benchmarking with companies around the globe. Two enterprises answered that it was not applicable. While MOIL Limited, BHEL and Mazagon Docks Ltd. did conduct international benchmarking.

Global benchmarking can be a good exercise for the enterprises which aspire to compete on the same level as its peers around the globe. This sort of benchmarking can also improve processes and standardisation internally as good practices and methods can be borrowed to improve themselves. However, more than 60 per cent of the enterprises did not conduct such a benchmarking.

Table 7.6

Global Benchmarking

Respondents	*Yes*	*No*	*No Answer*
15	3	10	2

Reducing Political Interference

To what extent has MoU reduced political interference in the management of your enterprise?

The MoU document is a method of reducing government control and increasing accountability in the enterprises. Therefore, reduction of political interference is a critical aspect of the MoU system.

Out of the 15 enterprises which answered the questionnaire, only 5 of the enterprises said that political interference has completely reduced. NHPC said that the reduction of political interference was partial. Two enterprises said that it made no difference. HUDCO said that political interference and MoU are not interdependent.

Table 7.7

Political Interference

Respondents	*Complete*	*Partial*	*No difference*
15	5	1	2

MoU and Organisational Effectiveness

When asked if MoU adequately measure performance in the areas of R&D, project implementation, HRD and other areas of organisational effectiveness, out of the 15 respondents 14 enterprises answered in affirmative that MoU adequately measures performance of the non-financial targets.

Non-financial targets are difficult to measure as they are not easily quantifiable. The MoU document seeks to objectively measure the performance of the enterprises based on these non-financial parameters. The MoU tries to find a balance between financial and non-financial targets when evaluating the performance of the enterprises and so it is very important that the MoU document adequately measures criteria like R&D, project implementation, HRD, and other areas of organisational effectiveness. All the enterprises felt that the MoU targets are adequately measured, indicating that the target setting for the non-financial indicators is adequate.

Table 7.8

Adequate Measure of Performance

Respondents	*Yes*	*No*	*No Answer*
15	14	0	1

MoU and Level Playing Field

A question was put to CPSEs if they feel that MoU is a fair agreement between the government and the enterprise, and if it provides a level playing field.

For any agreement to be effective there has to be a parity of obligations and responsibility between both the parties which enter into the agreement. The MoU system is an agreement that the government signs with the enterprise to ensure that the enterprise's performance is monitored/evaluated while relenting its control over the operations of the enterprise. So in essence, it is holding the enterprises accountable for their own performance and in exchange it promises to commit resources towards achieving the targets. If the government is not accountable for its commitments under this system, then the enterprise managers would be hard pressed to achieve their targets and the whole system would collapse. Therefore, it is essential that the MoU is a fair agreement which takes the interests of both the government and the enterprises into account.

Out of the 15 respondents, 11 of the enterprises felt that the MoU was a fair agreement and that the government is judged on its delivery to the commitments. While 3 enterprises felt that this was not the case and 1 enterprise did not answer the question. However, Mumbai Railway Vikas Corporation Ltd. (MRVC) said that even though the MoU is a fair agreement between the Government and the enterprise, the Government is never judged on its delivery on commitments which affects the performance of MoU.

Table 7.9

MoU as a fair agreement

Respondents	*Yes*	*No*	*No Answer*
15	11	3	1

RFMS-MoU

On being asked about the new RFMS-MoU system and if it will help in bringing about transparency and balance of information, the enterprises gave their views that since RFMS-MoU system will make the entire MoU framing, its submission, finalisation and evaluation process online, it may help reduce paper work and enhance transparency in the process. However, there was a concern that moving from paper-based system to paper-less system may take 2-3 years and it is very critical that the transition is smooth and acceptable by all stakeholders.

Performance Related Pay (PRP) and MoU

Introduction of PRP is an endeavour to motivate, retain and reward talent available in CPSEs. However, considering the complex and intricate environment in which the CPSEs function, forcing implementation of PRP based on a rigid and inflexible Bell Curve model is neither flexible nor desirable. Restriction of grading only 15 per cent of the executives as outstanding and 10 per cent of the executives every year as non-performers is a very challenging task. In fact, it questions the basic tenets of incentive and motivational theories. CPSEs fear that in the long run, the enterprises may have to face attrition and may give rise to some kind of industrial unrests. Most of them have therefore recommended that the 10 per cent of the compulsory grading of poor performers can be dispensed with.

CPSEs function in a very different environment, facing many challenges and constraints. One blanket scheme of PRP may not be applicable to all CPSEs. There may be a need to customise the scheme based on institutional requirements.

There is also a suggestion that the PRP amount must be proportional to the net profit of the enterprise rather than the present incremental scheme in vogue.

Factor Productivity of CPSEs

Another attempt has been made to study the performance of CPSEs in the context of the growth of the national economy. It is contended that, the index of TFP is the most appropriate criterion for evaluation, for it indicates the overall efficiency of resource utilisation by economic units over a specified time period. Productivity may be defined as the ratio between the production of a given commodity or service measured by volume, and one or more of the corresponding input factors, also measured by volume. The relation between an individual input factor and production is termed as the productivity of that individual factor.

According to Kendrick (1982):

> The chief means whereby humanity can raise itself out of poverty to a condition of relative material affluence is by increasing productivity. Productivity is the relationship between outputs of goods and services and the inputs of basic resources-labour,capital goods and natural resources.

In general productivity is defined as a measure of efficiency of transforming inputs into output. In fact, it is the ratio of output to input/s reflecting efficiency in factor use. The ratios of output to particular inputs are termed as partial productivities, whereas the ratio of output to a weighted sum of all the inputs used in the production process is defined as TFP. The partial productivities are simply the average products of the respective inputs, of which the simplest and most commonly used measure is labour productivity, capital productivity and raw material productivity. However, partial productivity has the limitations that it does not measure the overall productive efficiency of the economic unit. Hence in order to measure overall productive efficiency, TFP is being widely used. Accordingly, in the present analysis, average labour productivity, average capital productivity, average raw material productivity and average TFP is calculated for 44 listed CPSEs[1] in India during 1999-200 to 2013-14.

Measurement of Variables

In the present analysis, sale of goods and services has been taken as a measure of output. To calculate average labour productivity, average raw material productivity, average capital productivity variables like expenditure on salaries and wages and other employees benefits, expenditure on raw materials, stores and spares and net fixed assets respectively are used. Also in the analysis, ROI (return on investment) and ROE (return on equity) for the selected CPSEs have been calculated. The period of analysis is from 1999-2000 to 2013-14. The data used for the analysis is collected from the CMIE Prowess database.

Factor Productivity

Table 7.10 presents the average partial and TFP for the selected CPSEs used in the analysis. The factor productivity (average partial) and TFP are shown in Figures 7.1 and 7.2 respectively. It is observed from the analysis that the average productivity is higher of labour than of raw material and of raw material than of capital. From Table 7.10 we can see that the average productivity of labour during the analysis

1. List of the CPSEs used for analysis is provided in Annexure A-8.1..

period varies between a low of 16.58 in 2001-02 and a high of 34.77 in 2005-06. The lowest and the highest values of average productivity for capital are 2.27 in 2001-02 and 3.77 in 2013-14 and for raw material they are 3.11 in 2000-01 and 8.61 in 2013-14 respectively.

Table 7.10

Factor Productivity (Average Partial and Total) of CPSEs in India

Year	*Average Partial Raw Material Productivity*	*Partial Labour Productivity*	*Partial Capital Productivity*	*Total Factor Productivity*
1999-00	8.60	23.13	2.31	3.60
2000-01	3.11	18.07	2.31	3.64
2001-02	3.23	16.58	2.27	3.22
2002-03	3.50	20.32	2.40	3.46
2003-04	4.16	25.83	2.63	4.06
2004-05	4.60	28.25	3.10	4.20
2005-06	5.84	34.77	3.32	3.84
2006-07	5.25	32.75	3.62	4.38
2007-08	5.89	30.03	3.60	4.37
2008-09	6.61	31.17	3.60	4.33
2009-10	6.12	24.25	3.21	4.13
2010-11	8.39	20.33	3.33	4.21
2011-12	7.49	27.21	3.52	4.07
2012-13	6.72	24.60	3.68	4.05
2013-14	8.61	24.54	3.77	4.20

Source: Calculated from the CMIE Prowess Database.

Partial productivity values though useful for measuring the saving in particular input achieved over time, do not measure overall changes in productive efficiency, since they are affected by changes in the composition of input, i.e., by factor substitution. Therefore, TFP (total factor productivity) alone provides a measure for these overall changes in productive efficiency. It can be seen from Table 8.10 that TFP of selected CPSEs varies between 3.22 in 2001-02 to 4.38 in 2006-07. During the period of analysis, TFP has declined from 2007-2008 onwards.

Figure 7.1

Factor Productivity (Average Partial) of CPSEs in India

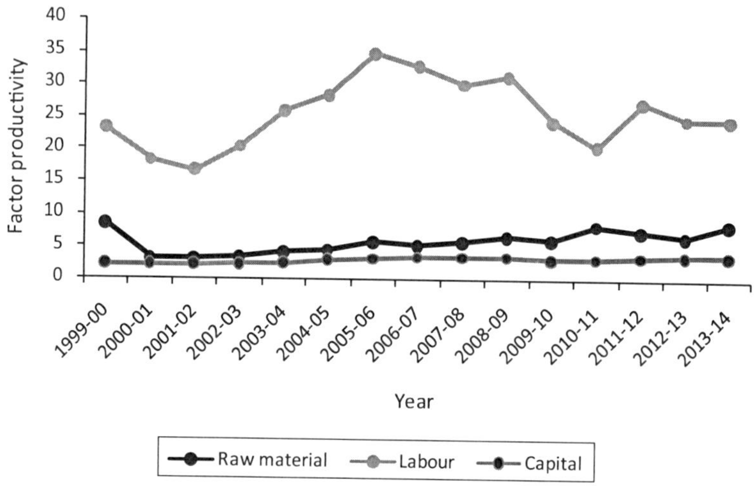

Figure 7.2

Total Factor Productivity of CPSEs in India

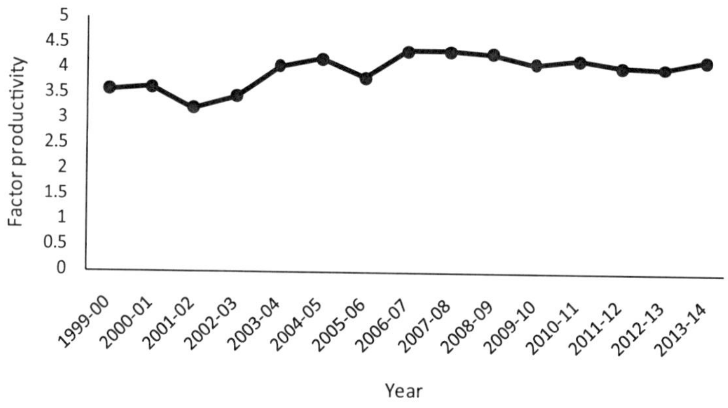

Return on Investment and Equity

Figure 7.3 presents the calculated ROI and ROE for the selected CPSEs. From the figure it is observed that both the measures of ROI and ROE have been increasing with fluctuations during the analysis period. It is observed from the analysis that the ROI of the selected CPSEs during the analysis period varies between a low of 12.02 per cent in 2013-14 and a high of 28.66 per cent in 2007-08 where as ROE varies between a low of 4.46 per cent in 2001-02 and a high of 45.27 per cent in 2008-09.

In general, the average partial productivities of labour, raw material, capital and average TFP are found to be greater than unity. This argues in favour of a further expansion in the production activities of the selected CPSEs. Also, the TFP of the selected CPSEs is found to be declining and hovering around 4 since a decade which is a concern. Both the calculated measures of ROI and ROE have been found to be increasing with fluctuations during the analysis period.

Figure 7.3

Calculated ROI and ROE for the Selected CPSEs

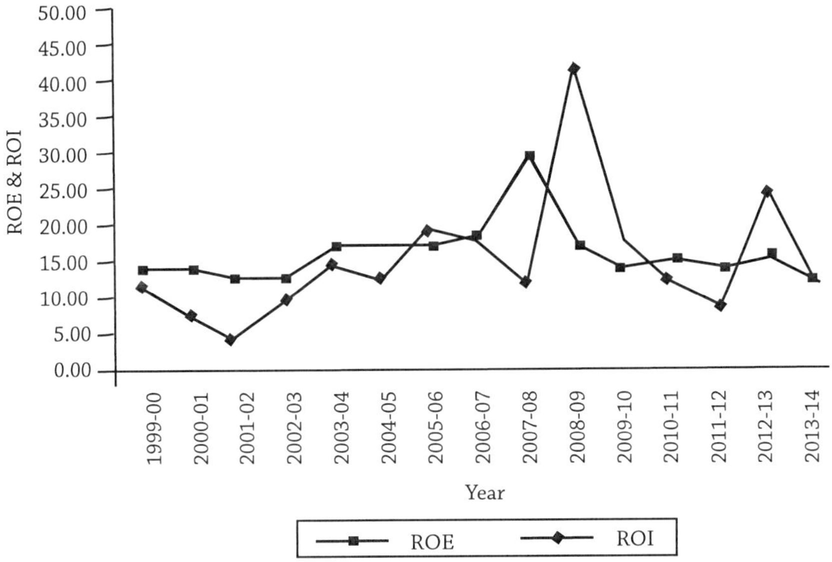

References

Kendrick, J.W. (1982). *Understanding Productivity: An Introduction to Dynamics Productivity Changes*. Baltimore, London: The John Hopkins University Press.

Mishra, R.K. and Geeta Potaraju (1999-2000). *Study of Memorandum of Understanding in Central Public Sector Enterprises in India*. Doctoral thesis by Geeta Potaraju to Osmania University under the guidance of Prof R K Mishra.

Annexure A-7.1

List of CPSEs Used in the Analysis

Andrew Yule & Co. Ltd.	*Indian Oil Corpn. Ltd.*
B E M L Ltd.	*M M T C Ltd.*
Balmer Lawrie & Co. Ltd.	*M O I L Ltd.*
Balmer Lawrie Invsts. Ltd.	*Mahanagar Telephone Nigam Ltd.*
Bharat Electronics Ltd.	*Mangalore Refinery & Petrochemicals Ltd.*
Bharat Heavy Electricals Ltd.	*N H P C Ltd.*
Bharat Immunologicals & Biologicals Corpn. Ltd.	*N M D C Ltd.*
Bharat Petroleum Corpn. Ltd.	*N T P C Ltd.*
Chennai Petroleum Corpn. Ltd.	*National Aluminium Co. Ltd.*
Coal India Ltd.	*National Buildings Construction Corpn. Ltd.*
Container Corpn. Of India Ltd.	*National Fertilizers Ltd.*
Dredging Corpn. Of India Ltd.	*Neyveli Lignite Corpn. Ltd.*
Engineers India Ltd.	*Oil & Natural Gas Corpn. Ltd.*
G A I L (India) Ltd.	*Oil India Ltd.*
H M T Ltd.	*Power Finance Corpn. Ltd.*
Hindustan Copper Ltd.	*Power Grid Corpn. Of India Ltd.*
Hindustan Fluorocarbons Ltd.	*Rashtriya Chemicals & Fertilizers Ltd.*
Hindustan Organic Chemicals Ltd.	*Rural Electrification Corpn. Ltd.*
Hindustan Petroleum Corpn. Ltd.	*S J V N Ltd.*
I T I Ltd.	*Scooters India Ltd.*
India Tourism Devp. Corpn. Ltd.	*Shipping Corpn. Of India Ltd.*
State Trading Corpn. Of India Ltd.	*Steel Authority Of India Ltd.*

8

Summary and Conclusion

Many countries around the globe have introduced PC (performance contracting) system as a tool to improve the functioning of their PSEs (public sector enterprises). It was in the late 1960s that the French government introduced PC system to provide operational autonomy and improve the enterprise performance. Countries like Bangladesh, China, Korea, Pakistan, Sri Lanka, Ghana, Gambia, Brazil, Argentina and many others have also experimented with this system. India too adopted a similar system and named it Memorandum of Understanding (MoU). This system was established as a result of the recommendations of Arjun Sengupta Committee set up in 1984, to analyse the performance of PSEs, and identify problems that they face and suggest measures for improving their functioning.

The Committee observed that the number of PSEs increased steadily in numbers and were visibly present spread all over the country and diversified from their focus on basic and heavy industry sector to areas of consumer goods, electronics, tourism and others. These enterprises were also employing around 2 million Indians during that period. Though there was a positive growth in terms of social objective, the fact remained that these enterprises were not performing well in terms of revenue generation and profits which became a matter of concern. The Committee recommended that to improve the performance the Central public undertakings the system of PC may be adopted and the enterprises may enter into agreements with their administrative ministries.

During the initial years of implementation only core sector enterprises entered into MoU with their ministries. The first set of MoU was signed by four CPSEs for the year 1987-88. Over the years, more CPSEs were brought within the system and in the year 2012-13 more than 157 CPSEs signed MoUs with their respective administrative ministries. The specific objective of the MoU system is to reduce the quantity of control and enhance the quality of accountability and putting in place the concept of management by objectives.

Box 8.1

Highlights of the Current MoU system

- MoU is an annual assessment method.
- It is a performance agreement between the enterprise and the concerned ministry.
- The main criteria for assessment of performance are financial and non-financial parameters.
- Targets are set at the beginning of the year (both financial and non-financial) based on which the enterprises are evaluated.
- The assessment in done on a 5 point rating scale.
- An institutional machinery is in place to oversee the implementation of MoU.
- Incentives linked with the MoU performance (PRP).

Revamping Initiatives

A number of initiatives have been taken by the Government of India (GoI) to improve and innovate the existing system of MoU. The first attempt to revamp the system was done in 2004-05 by the National Council of Applied Economic Research (NCAER). While the performance evaluation under the earlier system allocated 60 per cent weight to 'financial parameters' and 40 per cent weight to 'non-financial parameters', the NCAER recommended equal weights (50%) to both 'financial' and 'non-financial' parameters according to the Balanced Scorecard (BSC) approach to performance management. The financial parameters were to be presented in absolute values as well as ratios and the non-financial parameters were identified as: i) dynamic parameters, ii) enterprise-specific parameters, and iii) sector-specific parameters. In the year 2008, another review was undertaken on the functioning of MoU system and the Committee recommended that PEs (public enterprises) while determining its targets must take into consideration its performance of the past five years. It also recommended the need to consider risk factors which hinder the PEs to perform as per the fixed targets while evaluating an enterprise. Strengthening the role of task force members was also recommended by the Committee.

While declaring enterprises for excellence awards, the committee recommended the need to ensure that critical aspects of corporate governance are followed by the enterprise like composition of boards, frequency of meetings, audit process and customer interaction mechanisms etc.

In another attempt to refine the MoU system in the year 2011, Roongta Committee conducted a review and suggested various measures to improve the system. Revised formats were suggested for manufacturing and mining sectors, trading and consulting sectors, social sector, financial sector and sick enterprises. It was suggested that targets setting to be made more meaningful by benchmarking enterprises internationally as well as with the private sector. The report also recommended formulation of two additional enterprise specific parameters like physical production, globalisation, capital expenditure, expansion plans, economy measures to cut costs etc. The committee also recommended need to provide thrust on R&D (research & development).

In the year 2012, Mankad Committee was constituted to review the existing MoU guidelines and to make suitable recommendations to improve the system. The committee recommended exclusion of MoU system for sick and loss making units. The report recommended to provide discretionary powers to the task force and enough flexibility to decide on the basic target for enterprises signing MoU. As a part of the non-financial parameters elements like CSR (corporate social responsibility); sustainable development; productivity and internal processes;technology; R&D; quality; innovation; human resource management; project management and initiatives for growth were introduced.

We have come a long way with the system of MoU in India and this system has got stabilised over a period of time. A comprehensive system of performance linked incentive system was also put in place which is giving rich dividends and motivating employees and celebrating their success. All the committees referred above have reviewed the MoU system in terms of its formats, target setting process, benchmarking, incentivising, nature of financial and non-financial parameters etc.

At the national level, another major initiative unfolded. In order to effectively establish performance culture, the Government of India established a Performance Management Division (PMD) in the Cabinet Secretariat in January 2009. The key mandate of the PMD is to establish mechanisms for performance monitoring and performance evaluation in Government departments on a regular basis. It involves preparation of a Results Framework Document (RFD) by each department every year. The RFD highlights the departmental objectives and priorities for the current financial year as well as the achievements of the department against those pre-specified targets indicated in the RFD at the end of the year. Thus, RFD works as an accountability tool and provides the required focus by Government departments to deliver effectively and efficiently. It helps in bringing about objectivity to the working of Government departments and facilitates measurement of performance of the Government agencies so as to make necessary improvements wherever required. This system has provided an overarching framework of performance management for Government and MoU, which is a tool for enhancing enterprise performance, is also being integrated into this RFD system for making it sustainable and successful.

In the next section, we try to look at the MoU system and identify the areas of its convergence with RFD mechanism for PSEs and the initiatives taken by the Government to improve the system as a whole.

Aligning National Priorities and MoU Planning

PSEs are technology and labour intensive organisations and they require large amount of resources (both natural and human) for production purposes and processes. Does the MoU exercise generate a need for the Government/enterprise to prepare a master plan for resource allocation keeping the overall national picture/priorities in mind? For instance, in the case of steel plants during the MoU exercise, does at any point of time the Government assess availability of raw materials for various plants at different locations, availability of specialists, technology and R&D requirements and other issues of this nature. The point that we would like to raise here is does the system of MoU facilitate the emergence of a big picture on these critical issues? Another issue is that PEs develop various strategic planning documents like Corporate Plan, Annual Plan, and now also RFD. We need to bring in a sync between these multiple planning tools with MoU projections and align the system appropriately. This has been achieved to a great extent by the RFD system. It provides a mandate to the Government/ministries to prepare strategic plans considering the big picture and aligning enterprise performance and targets with the national priorities and goals.

Transparency and MoU System

Governments succeed when they establish transparent systems and effectively communicate the results to the public at large. Has MoU system achieved this objective? Are the results of the MoU system communicated to stakeholders so that they can assess the functioning of these enterprises? Some major initiatives have been taken by Government of India in the recent years in this direction. The MoU Division in the Department of Public Enterprises (DPE) through its website makes data available in the public domain. Ministry-wise/CPSE-wise information is made available along with CMIE projections for the company as well as a comparative picture of companies in similar sector are made available on the website. A novel feature of developing a critique on MoU by each enterprise, analysing the financial and non-financial parameters is also uploaded on the website. The summary of discussions during the negotiation meetings between the task force and the enterprise is also made available on the website. Effectively, a lot of information is being put up on the website to make the system transparent.

Performance management experts talk about the need to present data clearly and in a less complicated way (Kearney and Berman, 1999). It is a fact that people are interested in seeing government reports which provide them simple and clear information. People are interested in knowing not just good things but they also want to know about the challenges. Is MoU system addressing these issues adequately and is the data being presented to the public in this manner? In order to bring in transparency to the process, the MoU system which has been till date a manual process is being integrated into an online platform which is called the RFMS (Results Framework Management System) to make the system more efficient and fast. RFMS-MoU is an online system which has been developed by the DPE, Government of India, for the CPSEs/administrative ministries covered under the MoU system. This system will facilitate all the data to be made available online and will make the MoU system paperless. RFMS will also provide a platform for online discussion by CPSEs on various issues of MoU system. In the long run, MoU system is proposed to be integrated with the RFD system. The salient features of RFMS-MoU system are:

i) It is a user friendly internet based system allowing 24x7 processing of MoU.

ii) It is a single window (one stop shop) for all MoU related matters.

iii) It creates a paperless environment for processing of MoU activities.

iv) This system allows facility of creating a link among RFD of enterprises and administrative ministry.

v) This system allows dialogue between CPSE and administrative ministry to monitor performance of CPSEs from time-to-time.

Effectively communicating the performance of a PE to the public is essential. In India, the Right to Information (RTI) Act 2005 endeavours to bring in transparency in the functioning of Government agencies. The results have been mixed in the implementation of the Act.

South Korea has also developed an elaborate public disclosure system through The Official Information Disclosure Act in 1998 which requires that information on the operation of government agencies, SOEs (state owned enterprises) and public institutions to be disclosed. In addition, public institutions in Korea must also put up important information on their official websites in a prescribed manner by their strategy and finance ministry. The Korean system takes measures to avoid disclosure of false or insufficient information and also punitive actions in case of such cases for the employees and institutions. The government of South Korea gives penalty points to public institutions that have failed, are behind schedule or have incorrectly disclosed information. Penalties would be imposed on the people responsible for such a failure to disclose information and are required to submit plans to correct the problems that caused the failure in discloseing information. With the South Korean experience, we also need to strengthen implementation of RTI Act in India.

The other important issue here is does the MoU system support peer learning? There are many organisations which do good work in certain specific areas. Are organisations leaning from each other's good work and replicating the same in their organisations? Are we learning from best practices at least within the national context?

MoU and Incentivising Performance

One of the most challenging aspects of a PMS (performance management system) is the component of inter-enterprise comparison. In the case of MoU, the process provides opportunity for incentivising and rewarding good performance and provides ample opportunities for celebrating achievement and success. Indian system of MoU is a very good example of how excellent and good performing SOEs are provided financial and non-financial incentives, which motivate them for further improvements. Designing consequences for non-performance is very challenging. One of the major challenge that MoU system faces is that it becomes very difficult to pin-point exact reasons for non-performance and therefore making people accountable for not discharging their responsibilities becomes difficult.

The South Korean experience with PC may be of particular interest while designing consequences for non-performing enterprises. The Government in Korea has been very successful in evolving a sophisticated and comprehensive incentive system of performance related bonuses over the last 30 years. As a result, the variation in bonuses received by the SOEs in South Korea has increased steadily. The Korean system also identifies under-performing PEs and imposes penalties. PEs which perform poorly receive warnings from the government along with additional cuts in bonuses. Such PEs are also obligated to submit a plan for turn-around or improving their performance. Public recognition is in itself a strong incentive or penalty system in Korea as it is carries great import in their society. Therefore, the government sanctions coupled with non-material sanctions ensures that PEs will try to perform better. In India, we must similarly try to identify non-pecuniary rewards or penalties to ensure hard work and performance of non-performing PEs and to create a fine balance between incentivising good performance and strengthening under-performance.

Performance Criteria and Benchmarking

A paper written by Kearney and Berman (1999) raises critical issues with regard to choice of performance measures. Selection of performance measures is critical as it decides the usefulness of data and whether it serves the purpose or not. A good example is the number of tonnes of refuse collected per day is a measure used by the local government, and to achieve this goal the workers may work hard and reach the target. But if the policy makers/public are interested not only in the collection of refuse but also want to know how well it is collected and is it left in a place that is close to their neighbourhood or the amount of pollution that it generates, this might result in public anger with Government and the employees will be left feeling unappreciated.

This may as well be true with MoU system, especially enterprises involved in mining and construction sector Such enterprises use natural resources, and many a times there could be a conflict arising in terms of whether the resources belong to a protected zone? Are they confining to environmental rules and regulations? Or are they creating environmental hazards? Are we thinking about all these issues?

As per the latest guidelines 2013-14, enterprises need to benchmark their performance with peer companies, at national and global levels, and they must be in sync with targets given by Planning Commission, Ministry of Finance etc. Target setting process is the lifeline of a PC system in PEs. The question that arises here is do the enterprises have the capacity to take up the benchmarking activities? There is a long standing demand for setting up an expert group at the DPE/ministry level to take up the process of target setting and looking at enterprises sector-wise. This has yet not been achieved and enterprises are left to take up this activity on their own.

Conclusion

After many decades of existence of public sector in India, there are still many questions unanswered. We have to go a long way to achieve the objective of setting up a socialistic pattern of society and there is practically no concrete evidence on improvements in human development indicators at the national and state levels. Though the Government has delegated financial and administrative powers to PEs to a great extent to provide considerable financial leverage for taking prudent decisions, the results are not satisfactory. It has been several decades since the MoU system has been introduced in India in the hope of incentivising performance, yet there are a considerable number of PEs which are languishing in the fair and good category in terms of performance. Despite these efforts there are performance challenges that exist in PSEs which are mainly due to inadequate systems, processes, and latest technology. Setting in an appropriate performance culture is the key for any major improvements to be visibly seen. Change in cultural aspects and mindsets are the key for any success in this direction. Greater transparency in the operation of the PEs coupled with using data for effective decision-making are areas of concern. However, there is a clear direction that has been set with the Performance Management Division taking lead and rolling out the overarching PMS and implementing RFD. The RFD system provides a comprehensive framework of performance measurement and management for all the government departments/ministries, to develop performance plans in sync with the national priorities and programmes. With the RFD system in place, it will give greater stability to the MoU system and make it sustainable.

References

Government of India (1984). *Report of the Committee to Review Policy for Public Enterprises* (Arjun Sengupta Committee Report). New Delhi.

————. (2008). *Report of the Working Group on Review of MoU Guidelines CPSEs* (Ashok Chandra Report). New Delhi.

————. (2012). *Report on the Committee on the MoU System* (Mankad Committee Report). New Delhi.

Kearney, Richard and Evan Berman (eds.) (1999). *Public Sector Performance: Management, Motivation, and Measurement (Classics on Cassette)*. Boulder, CO: Westview Press.

Kim, Junki (n.d.). *State Owned Enterprise Reforms and Corporate Governance Reforms in South Korea.* Graduate School of Public Administration, Seoul University.

Mishra, R.K., R. Nandagopal, P. Geeta and B. Navin (2002). Role of MoU in Public Enterprises Reforms. Chennai: Vikas Publications.

National Council of Applied Economic Research (2004). *Study on the Revamping of MoU System.* New Delhi.

Park, Young C. (1986). "A System for Evaluating the Performance of Government Invested Enterprises in the Republic of Korea', in Prajapati Trivedi (ed.) (1992), *Memorandum of Understanding: An Approach to Improving Public Enterprise Performance.* New Delhi: International Management Publishers. p.523.

Planning Commission (2011). *Report of Panel of Experts on Reforms in Central Public Sector Enterprises* (Roongta Committee Report). New Delhi: Government of India.

Powell, S. (2004). "The Challenges of Performance Measurement", *Management Decision* 42(8): 1017-23.

Trivedi, Prajapati (1989). "Performance Evaluation System for Memoranda of Understanding", *Economic and Political Weekly* XXIV(21), May 1989. (Also reprinted in the *Institute of Public Enterprise Journal* XII(2), June 1989.)

Documents:

Annexure–I to OM (RFMS-MoU), No.3(15)2013-DPE(MoU), dated 2014.

Memorandum (RFMS-MoU), Circular No.3 (15)2013-DPE (MoU), Government of India, Ministry of Heavy Industries & Public Enterprises, DPE, New Delhi, 2014.

Public Enterprise Survey (2011-12). Department of Public Enterprise, Government of India,New Delhi.

2012 Modularization of Korea's Development Experience (2013), 'Governance of SOEs and Public Institutions in Korea', Professor, KDI School of Public Policy and Management, IlChong Nam.

Annexure A-1

List of CPSEs who Responded to the Questionnaire

1	MOIL Limited
2	Engineers India Limited
3	NMDC Limited
4	Housing and Urban Development Corporation Ltd.
5	NHPC Limited
6	Bharat Dynamics Ltd.
7	Bharat Heavy Electricals Limited (BHEL)
8	India Rare Earths Limited
9	Mazagon Docks Limited
10	RailTel Corporation of India Ltd
11	Mumbai Railway Vikas Corporation Ltd. (MRVC).
12	PEC Ltd.
13	Hindustan Antibiotics Ltd
14	Instrumentation Limited
15	Neyveli Lignite Corporation Limited

Annexure A-2

Questionnaire for the Evaluation of the MoU System[1]

General Questions

1. Name of the enterprise?
2. Category of enterprise
3. The year in which the enterprise entered into MoU with the Government?
4. Indicate the ratings obtained by your enterprise in the years of signing MoU?

Year	*Grade*	*Rank*
2003		
2004		
2005		
2006		
2007		
2008		
2009		
2010		
2011		
2012		
2013		

5. What are various methods of planning processes in the enterprise?
6. How do you align the MoU plan with the other plans (corporate Plan, RFD, and other strategic plans and production targets)? Explain
7. Has the financial delegation of powers to CPSEs facilitated the enterprise to take investment decisions in a faster and smoother manner? Yes/No
8. Do you feel that MoU has helped the enterprise secure greater accountability at the various levels? Yes/No
9. Has the MoU system helped your enterprise to increase commitment to various departments and individuals? Yes/No
10. What is your view on the MoU guidelines released by the DPE each year? Do you think that the MoU formats help enterprises to design the MoU appropriately? What are the suggestions you have in this regard?
11. What is the procedure for target setting in your enterprise? Explain
12. Who are all involved in the process of target setting?

---

1. Please respond to the questionnaire and send it to the following:
Dr Geeta Potaraju, Assistant Professor, Institute of Public Enterprise (IPE), Hyderabad. Email: *pgeeta@ipeindia.org.*
Mr Pranav Garimella, Research Intern, IPE, Hyderabad, Email: *pranav.garimella88@gmail.com*

13. Is there any technical expertise drawn from outside to take up this activity? Yes /No
14. If yes, give details
15. Does the enterprise conduct benchmarking exercise with similar companies in India?
16. Does the enterprise conduct benchmarking exercise with companies around the globe? Explain the process
17. To what extent has the MoU reduced political interference in the management of your enterprise? Partial / Complete / No difference
18. Should the duration of the MoUs be fixed as per the nature of sector-enterprise specific? Please justify the need for extending the duration?
19. What according to you are the best indicators of financial performance?

Year	Criteria	Performance
	Gross margin/gross block	
	Net profit/net worth	
	Gross profit/capital employed	
	Gross margin	
	Gross sales	
	PBDIT/total employment	
	Added value/sales	

20. Do you think the current system of setting financial criteria in a uniform manner fair for your enterprise? Please explain
21. Should the financial criteria be sector specific? Yes/No
22. What according to you are the best indicators of non-financial performance?
23. In your view can the non-financial parameters be objectively measured? Do you think the enterprise specific parameters need to be strengthened/given more weightage?
24. Does MoU adequately measure performance in the areas of R&D, project implementation, HRD, and other areas of organizational effectiveness? Yes/No
25. Does the PRP system provide adequate reward/motivation to employee? Do you have any suggestions to improve the existing system?
26. Do you feel that MoU is a fair agreement between the government and the enterprise? Does it provide a level playing field? Is the Government judged on its delivery to the commitments? Yes/ no
27. If no, why?
28. Please give your views on the new RFMS-MoU system? Will this system help in bringing about transparency and balance of information? Please illustrate the issues with examples?

Annexure A-3[2]

Questionnaire for the Valuation of the MoU System: Ad-Hoc Task Force[3]

Name: **Syndicate:**

1. As an Ad-Hoc Task Force (ATF) are you given sufficient time to prepare for the review an enterprise? Please elaborate your experience.
2. Does the Task Force receive sufficient amount of information well in advance from the enterprises including the macro functioning and/or micro functioning of the enterprise in order to negotiate effectively with the enterprises? Please explain the challenges and suggest ways for improvements.
3. Does the task force receive periodic (quarterly/half yearly) updates on the performance of the enterprise? Kindly explain how such periodic performance reports will help the task force members to better prepare for the target setting process?
4. Are factors like capital, market forces, resources and global economic trends considered when setting targets for enterprises? Please elaborate. Suggest any innovations that can be incorporated to this target setting process.
5. What is the role of the task force in the negotiation of targets? Is there sufficient information available with the task force members on the problems, processes and technical aspects of the enterprises before the negotiation process starts? Please elaborate.
6. Please give your opinion on the current system of assigning weightages to financial and non-financial parameters under the MoU system? Is there a need to change the policy to introduce sector specific weightages for enterprises?
7. Do the uniform formats for MoUs prepared by the DPE need to be changed to sector specific formats? If yes, what changes can be brought about in the format of MoUs for public enterprises in your syndicate?
8. What effect has the introduction of the Results Framework Document (RFD) system had on the working of the MoU system? Is it complementing the MoU system? If no, how is it affecting the working of the MoU system?
9. Suggest any improvements that can be made to the present system of MoU. What is the future of the performance management system? Will the MoU system be relevant even if the government considers disinvestment of public sector?
10. Does the task force consider experiences from other countries to bolster the performance contracting system in India? If yes, please provide specific instance of task force members borrowing from international experience/best practices.

---

2. IPE, Osmania University Campus, Hyderabad.

3. Please respond to the questionnaire and send it to the following:
Dr Geeta Potaraju, Assistant Professor, IPE, Hyderabad. Email: *pgeeta@ipeindia.org.*
Mr Pranav Garimella, Research Intern, IPE, Hyderabad, Email: *pranav.garimella88@gmail.com*

Select Subject Bibliography

Books

Jones, Leroy P. (1982). *Public Enterprise in Less Developed Countries*. Cambridge University Press.

Mishra, R.K., Nandgopal, Geeta P and Navin Bulusu (2001). *Role of Memorandum of Understanding in Public Enterprise Reforms*. New Delhi: Vikas Publications.

Sethi, Krishen G. and Waris R. Kidwai (1990). *What and How of Memorandum of Understanding*. New Delhi: Scope Publication.

Trivedi, Prajapathi (1990). *Memorandum of Understanding: An approach to Improving Public Enterprise*. International Management Publisher.

Articles/Papers

Bhat, K.S. (2002). "Holding Company and Memorandum of Understanding", in R.K. Mishra, Nandgopal, Geeta P and Navin Bulusu (2001). *Role of Memorandum of Understanding in Public Enterprise Reforms*. New Delhi: Vikas Publications.

Green, Diana (1982). "Government and Industry in France: A Contractual Approach", in *Public Money* 2(2), September.

Ghosh, Utpal (1997). "The MoU and Performance of Central PSEs", *Occasional Paper* No. 1. Department of Public Enterprise, Ministry of Industry, GoI.

Gunasekar, Sangeeta and Jayati Sarkar (2014). *Does Autonomy Matter in State Owned Enterprises? Evidence from Performance Contracts in India*. Mumbai: IGIDR.

Mathur, B.L. and Reeta Mathur (2010). "Accountability and Autonomy Relationship in Central Public Sector Enterprises through MoU", Paper presented in the *International Conference on Applied Economics ICOAE*.

Murthy, K.R.S. (1990). "MoU: More Memorandum than Understanding", *Economic and Political Weekly*, 26 May 26.

Nellis, John R. (1989). "Contract Plans and Public Enterprise Performance", *World Bank Discussion Papers*.

Obongo, Sylvester Odhiambo (2009). "Implementation of Performance Contracting in Kenya", *International Public management Review* 10(2).

Ramamurthy, Ravi (1983). *Methods for Controlling Public Enterprises: International Comparisons*. Report on Industry and Development No.7. Vienna: UNIDO.

———. (1986). *Performance Contracting System in Bangladesh*. Report submitted to Finance Ministry, Government of Bangladesh and UN project No. BCD/82/033.

Sankar, T.L., R.K. Mishra, Nandagopal (1991). "Do State Level Public Enterprises Need Memorandum of Understanding?", *Economic and Political Weekly:* M93.

Sharma, Sreedhar J. (1982). "The Enterprise Contract System in Public Enterprise Management: The French Experience", *Journal of Institute of Public Enterprise* 5(4): 62-76, October-December.

Shirley, Mary (1983). ""Contracts between the State and its Enterprises: The Experience of Senegal", *World Bank Staff Working Paper* No.577. Management and Development Series. Washington.

————. (1996). "Enterprise Contracts: A Route to Reform", *Finance And Development*, September.

————. (1998). *Why Performance Contracts for State Owned Enterprises Haven't Worked.* World Bank Group. Private Sector. August.

Shirley, Mary and Lexin Colin Xu (2000). *Empirical Effects of Performance Contracts Evidence from China.* OECD.

————. (2000a). *Corporate Governance of SOEs in China.* Paper presented at OECD meeting at China. 18-19 January.

Trivedi, Prajapathi (1987). "Sengupta Report on Public Enterprises Eloquent Fuzziness at its Best", *Economic and Political Weekly* 22(22).

————. (1988). "Theory and Practice of the French Contracts for Improving Public Enterprise Performance: Some Lessons for LDCs", *Public Enterprise* 8(1), January.

————. (1989). Performance Evaluation System for Memorandum of Understanding", *Economic and Political Weekly* 24(21): M55-M59.

————. (1990). "Lack of Understanding on Memorandum of Understanding", *Economic and Political Weekly* 25(47).

————. (1990a). "Memorandum of Understanding and Other Performance Improvement Systems: A Comparison", *The Indian Journal of Public Administration* XXXVI(2), April-June.

————. (1990b). "Memorandum of Understanding: Methodological Issues Relating to Recent Policy Changes", *Indian Management* 29(7). Quarterly Journal of the All India Management Association.

Trivedi, Prajapathi and Suresh Kumar (1989). "Memorandum of Understanding: A Case Study of the Indian Airlines Experience". Bureau of Public Enterprise. June. (*Mimeo*),

Trivedi, Prajapathi and Sunil Kumar (1990). "Memorandum of Understanding and the Korean Performance Evaluation System", *The Journal of Institute of Public Enterprise* 13(2), April-June.

Trivedi, Prajapathi and M.P. Vithal (1992). "Menu of Financial Indicators Used in MOUs: An Exercise in Clarification", *Economic and Political Weekly* 27(22).

Venkatesan, R. (1989). "Memorandum of Understanding and Business Performance Appraisal of the Public Sector", *Economic and Political Weekly.*

Vithal, Panduranga (2000). "Internationalization of MoU by PEs", *Institute of Public Enterprise Journal* 23(3&4).

Reports

Report of the Working Group on Review of MoU Guidelines in CPSEs. Submitted to Department of Public Enterprise, Government of India, New Delhi, 2008.

Report of Panel of Experts on Reforms in Central Public Sector Enterprises (CPSEs). Submitted to Department of Public Enterprise, Government of India, New Delhi, 2011.

Report of the Committee on the MoU System. Submitted to Department of Public Enterprise, Government of India, New Delhi, 2012.

Study on the Revamping of the MoU System. A Report submitted by National Council of Applied Economic Research to Department of Public Enterprise, Government of India, New Delhi, 2004.

The Belgian State as a Shareholder: A Comparison with International Best Practices and OECD Guidelines on Corporate Governance for State Owned Enterprises. Centre Public Governance, Guberna, March 2014.

Newspapers

Trivedi, Prajapathi (1990). "So What's New with the MoU", *Financial Express*, Bombay. 7 May.

———. (1991). "Memorandum of Understanding Means to Weigh Real Corporate Ability", *Business Standard*, Calcutta. 27 March.

———. (1991a) "MoU and Privatisation (Substitutes or Complements)", *Business India*, 4-17 March.

———. (1992). "Will the MoU System Work", *Financial Express*, Calcutta. March.

Thesis/Other material

Mishra, R.K. (undated). *Memorandum of Understanding for State and Central Public Sector Enterprises in India.* Training Programme Material. Hyderabad: Institute of Public Enterprise, OU Campus.

P., Geeta (2000). *Memorandum of Understanding and Public Enterprises in India.* Phd Theses. Submitted to Department of Business Management and Commerce, Osmania University, Hyderabad.

Rath, A.K. (2010). *Report on Activities Related to Performance of CPSEs.* Gurgaon: Management Development Institute. Sinha, R K. (undated). *MoU: A Handbook for Policy Makers.* Pamphlet. ASCI Library.

Trivikram, K. (undated) *MoU Some Reflections.* Training Programme Material. Hyderabad: Institute of Public Enterprise, OU Campus.